Whimsical
GIRLS

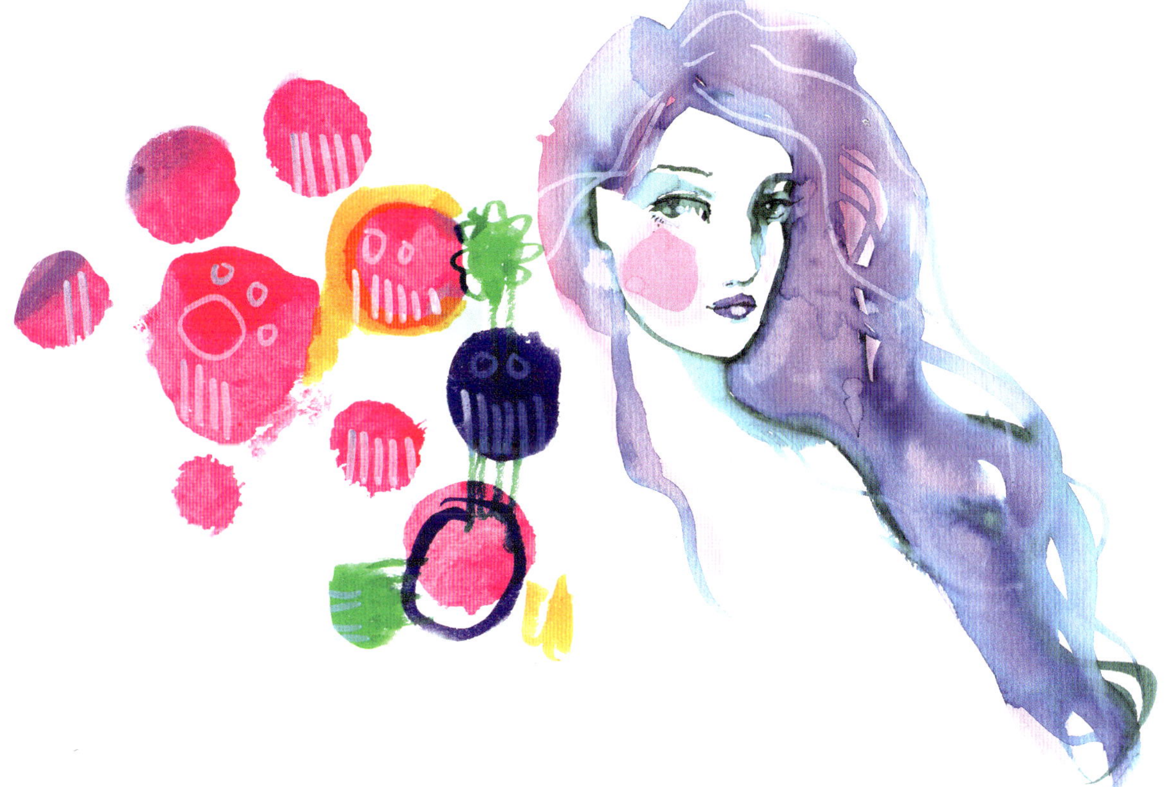

This book is dedicated to

the most whimsical
and lovely girls in the world,
Ruby and Sophie.
I love drawing with you and hope we
keep on creating together forever.
With oodles of love from a very biased

Aunty Jane

Get Creative 6
An imprint of Mixed Media Resources
104 West 27th Street
New York, NY 10001

Copyright © 2018 by Jane Davenport

All rights reserved. No part of this publication may be reproduced or used in any form or by any means—graphic, electronic, or mechanical, including photocopying, recording, or information storage-and-retrieval systems—without permission of the publisher.

The designs in this book are intended for the personal, noncommercial use of the retail purchaser and are under federal copyright laws; they are not to be reproduced in any form for commercial use. Permission is granted to photocopy content for the personal use of the retail purchaser.

ISBN: 978-1-64021-014-1

Manufactured in China

3 5 7 9 10 8 6 4

First Edition

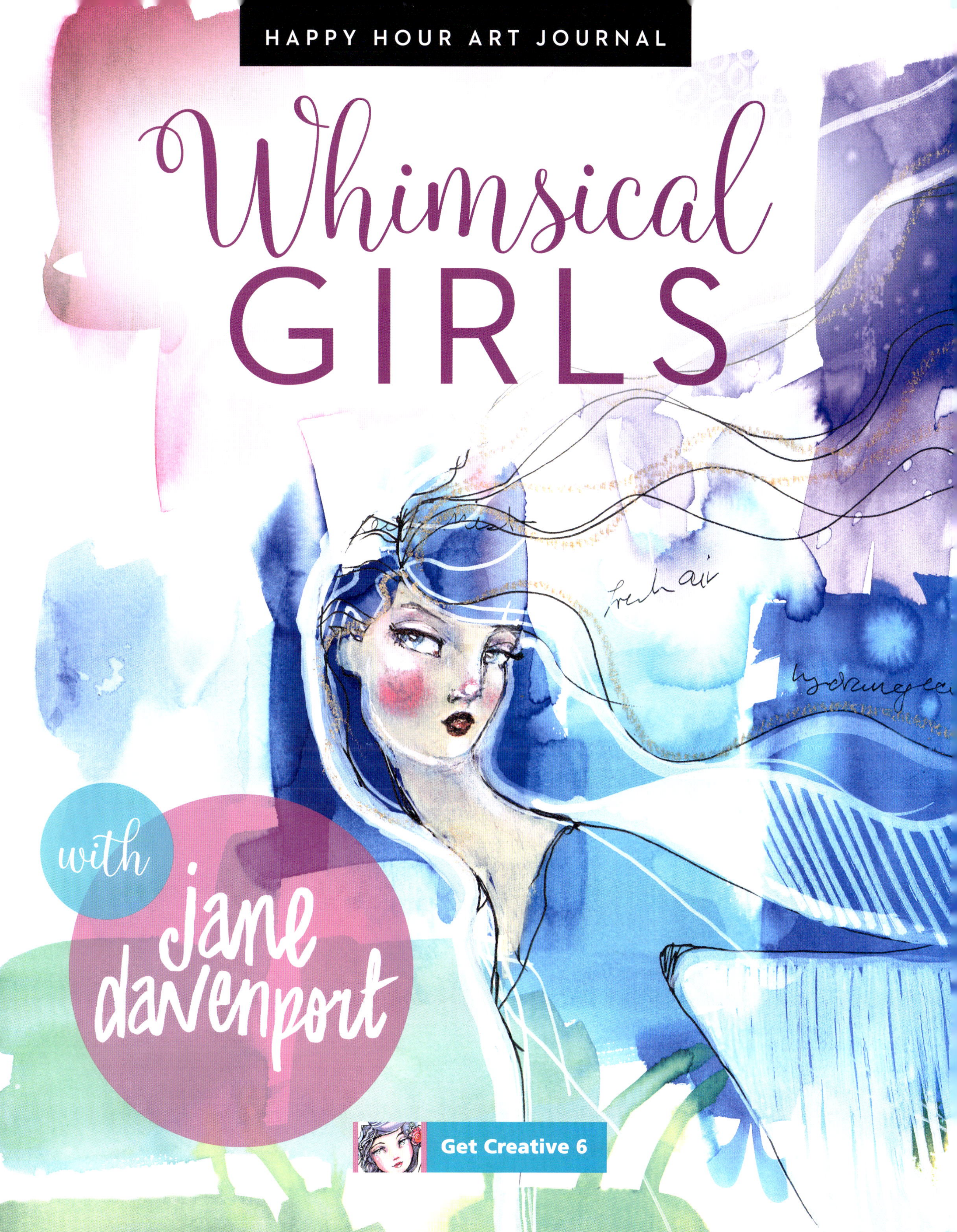

HAPPY HOUR ART JOURNAL

Whimsical
GIRLS

with

jane
davenport

Get Creative 6

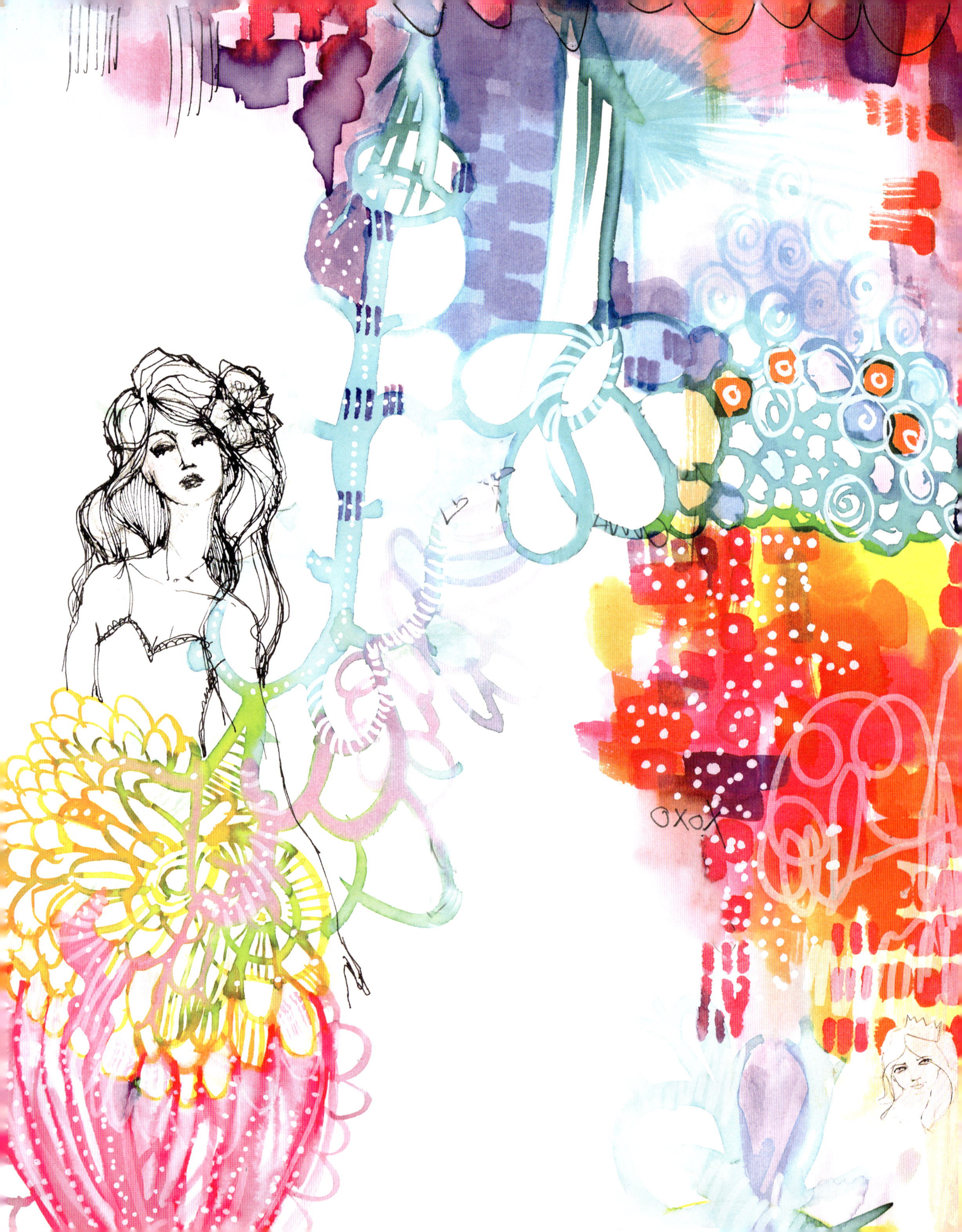
xoxo

Introduction

You and I are probably pretty similar in that we lead very busy lives, and fitting in art time can be a challenge. I passionately believe that creativity is important and that squeezing in even a few minutes every day can help make you feel more balanced. When you add up the minutes of coloring, painting, and drawing from your week, they may equal "Happy Hour"!

I create in an art journal every day. The thing about an art journal is that it's not about the outcome, it's all about the process. So it really does not matter a jot if you "mess up." There are no rules in art, so there's nothing to break. There are just lessons to learn about color and line and what makes you happy. It's so freeing!

I have designed this book so you can add your own style and sensibilities. You can simply add color, but how you do that is up to you! You can draw in extra details. Why not tear and cut shapes from the collage papers and glue them in as new backgrounds?

The mix of papers encourages the use of mixed media (which simply means using anything you want!). My wish for you is to unwind and have fun while building your creative confidence.

If you already keep an art journal, then I hope you enjoy playing with me in this one. And if you have never kept an art journal, I hope that you love this experience and feel inspired to do more!

Join me at janedavenport.com for more ideas, tips, and techniques.

I really treat my journals like a lab to experiment in. So anything goes!

jane davenport

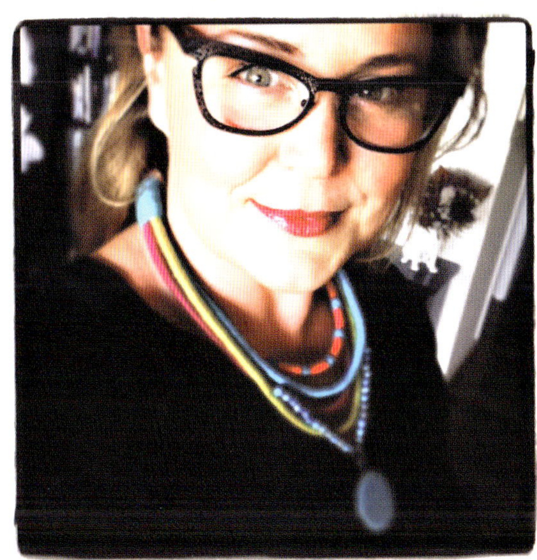

ABOUT JANE

Jane Davenport is an artist, best-selling author, workshop leader, and creative director of her own line of art supply products. In her spare time, she is an avid art supply junkie, art journal evangelist, and koala mama (yes, koalas visit her garden!).

After studies in Paris, Jane began her career as a fashion illustrator. She went on to become a textile designer, fashion designer, runway photographer, and gallery owner. Through owning the gallery, she discovered a love of teaching and now shares her passion and knowledge with thousands of students through her online workshops.

She and her husband, Gus, live in Byron Bay, Australia, with their three small dogs. She is the author of *I ♥ Drawing: Fabulous Figures*.

JANEDAVENPORT.COM

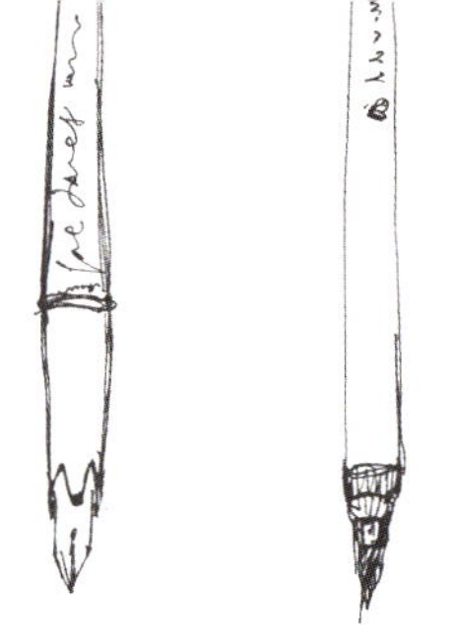
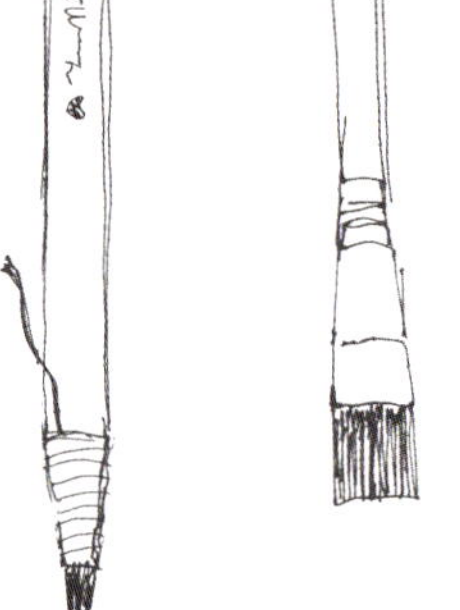
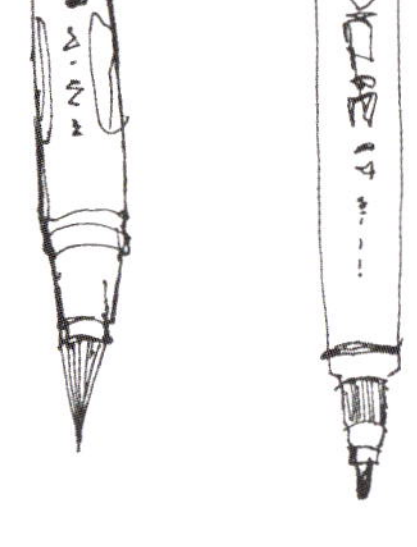
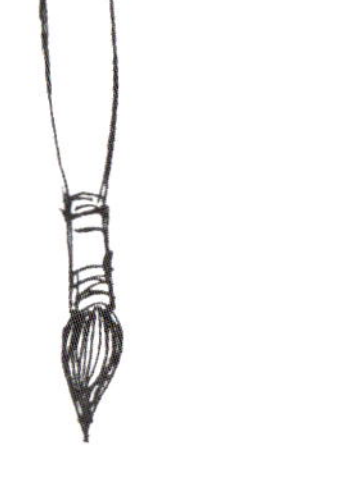
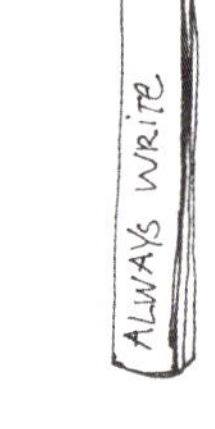

How to use this book

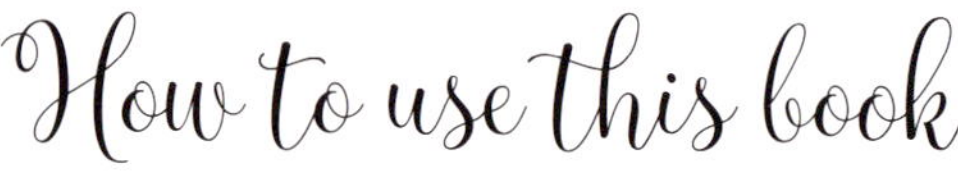

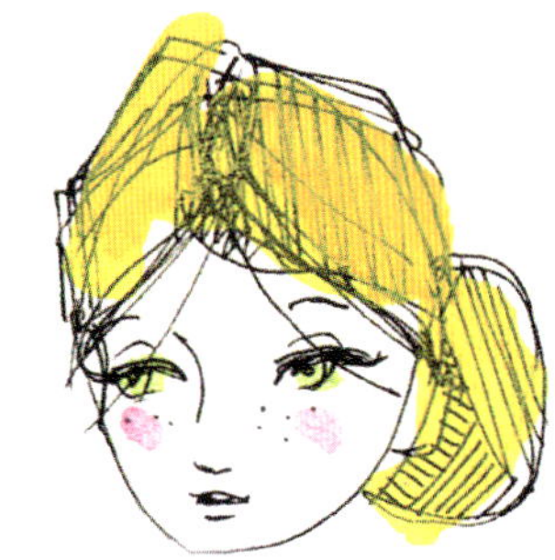

On the right-hand side of each spread is artwork for you to co-create with me. Most of the images are black-and-white line drawings, while some have more shading to give you a head start in adding depth to your artwork. On the left side is artwork from my own journals that I hope will spark ideas and inspire your own creations. This is an art journal, which means it is for your own personal enjoyment. So let loose and just have fun with color and creativity!

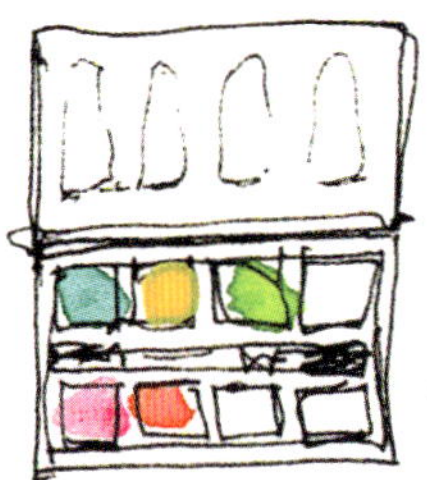

There are six types of creative papers in this book. If you look at the inside margin of each spread you'll see the type of paper. Below I suggest media to use with each. The pages are perforated so you can remove them to work on or pull them out when you're finished.

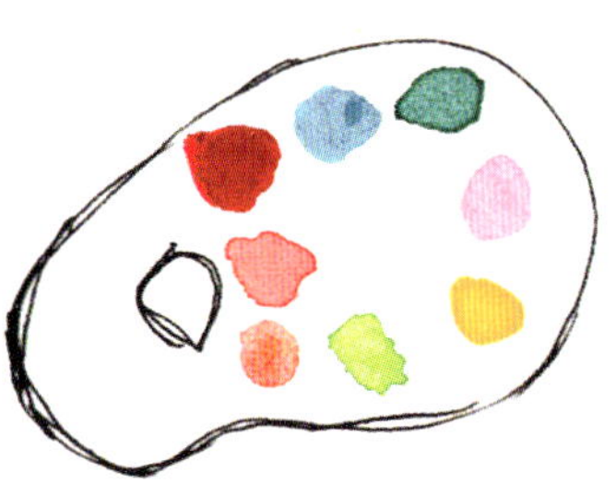

Coloring paper. This smooth wood-free paper is wonderful for colored pencils, pens, and other dry media.

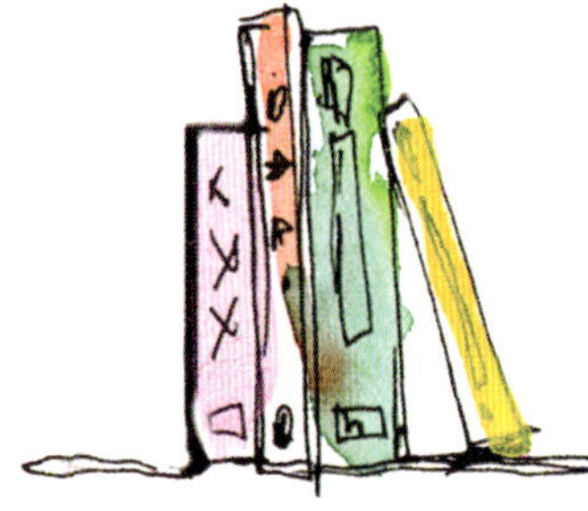

Kraft paper. This colored paper works great with pencil, markers, paint pens, gouache, and acrylic paint. Colors leap out of the toned paper. It will wrinkle if it gets too wet, which I find charming, but you may not, so just be aware of its limitations!

Marker paper. A slightly heavier, smooth wood-free paper that can take more marker without bleeding through too much. It's great for most media, but it's not intended for wet media, so go lightly with water.

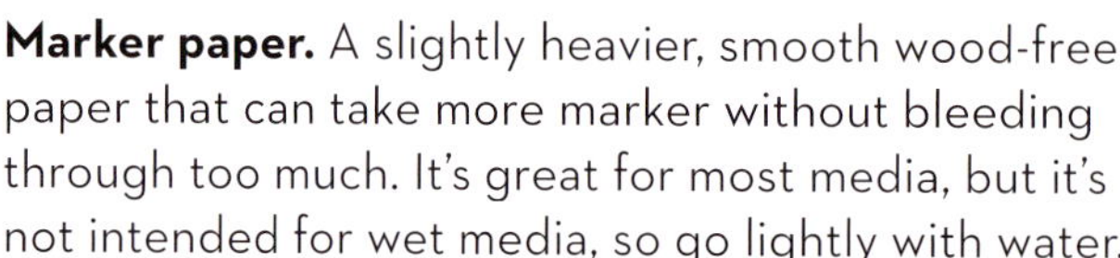
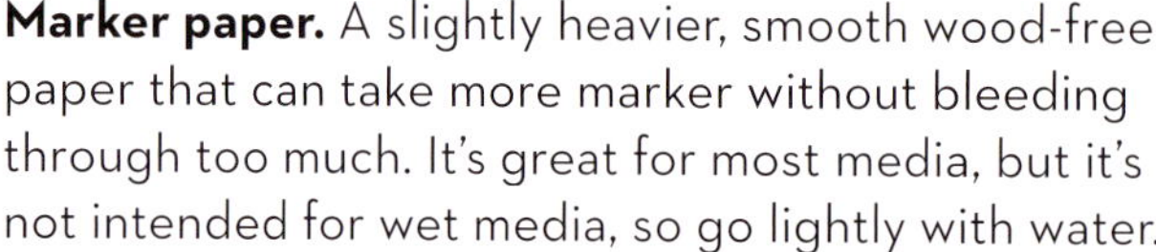
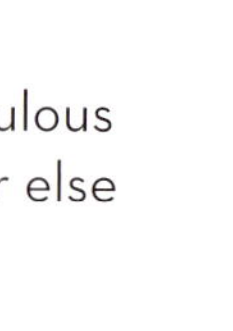
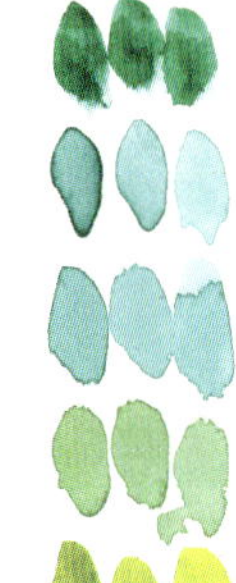

Watercolor paper. This heavyweight paper is fabulous not only for watercolors but for inks and whatever else you want to use.

Collage paper. A lightweight, origami-style paper that you can cut or tear up to use as collage paper. Glue it down with a good ol' glue stick or matte medium.

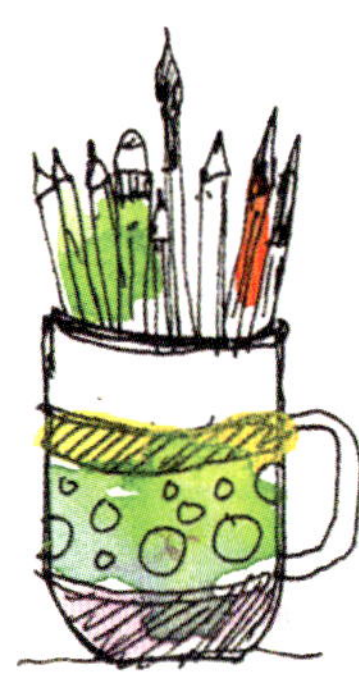
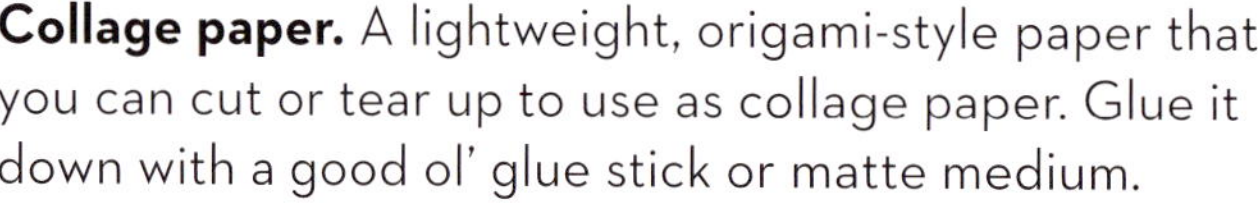

Sticker sheet. Everyone loves stickers (especially me!). Use them in this book or in your other art journals.

Stamp, draw, paint, daub, spritz, and splash!

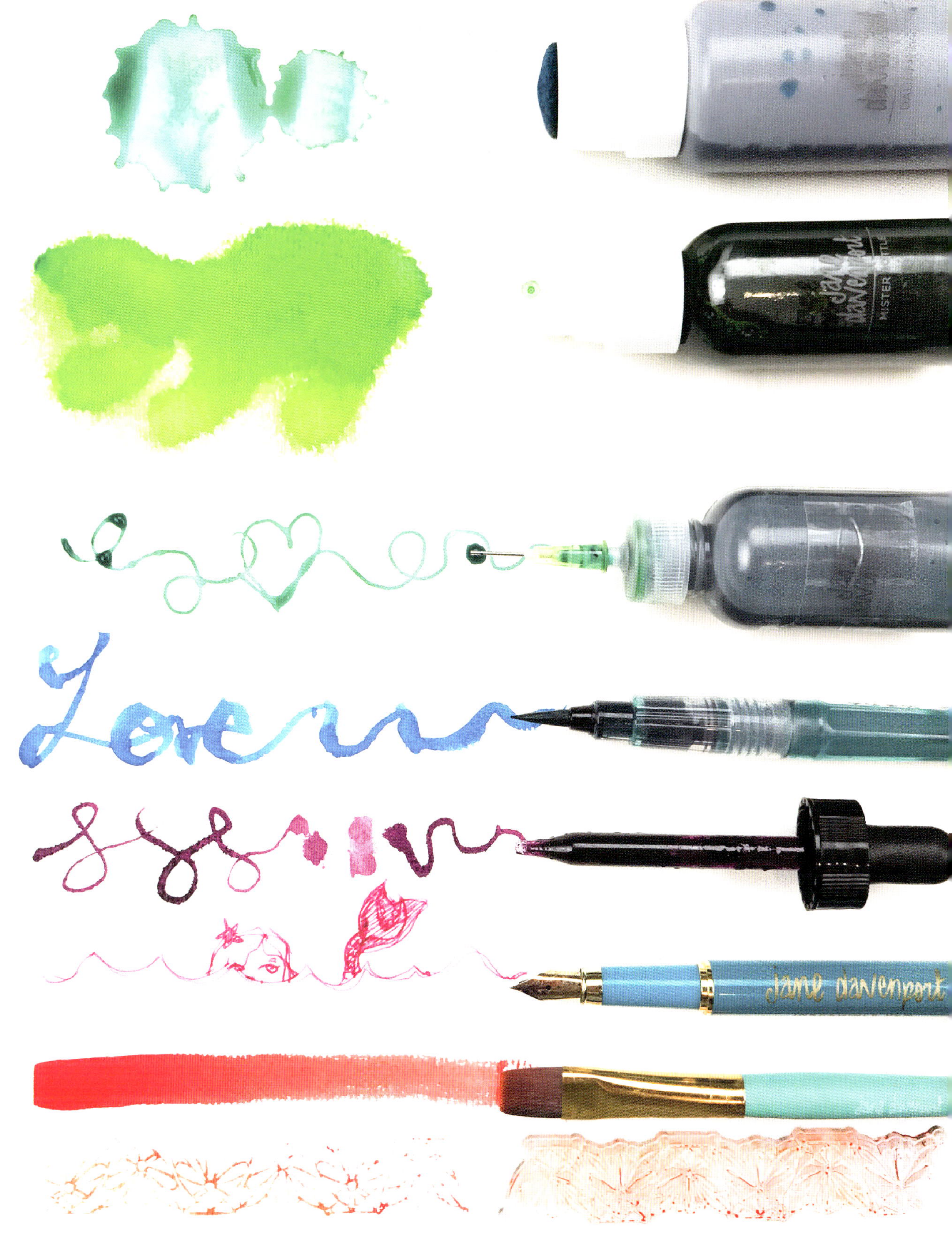

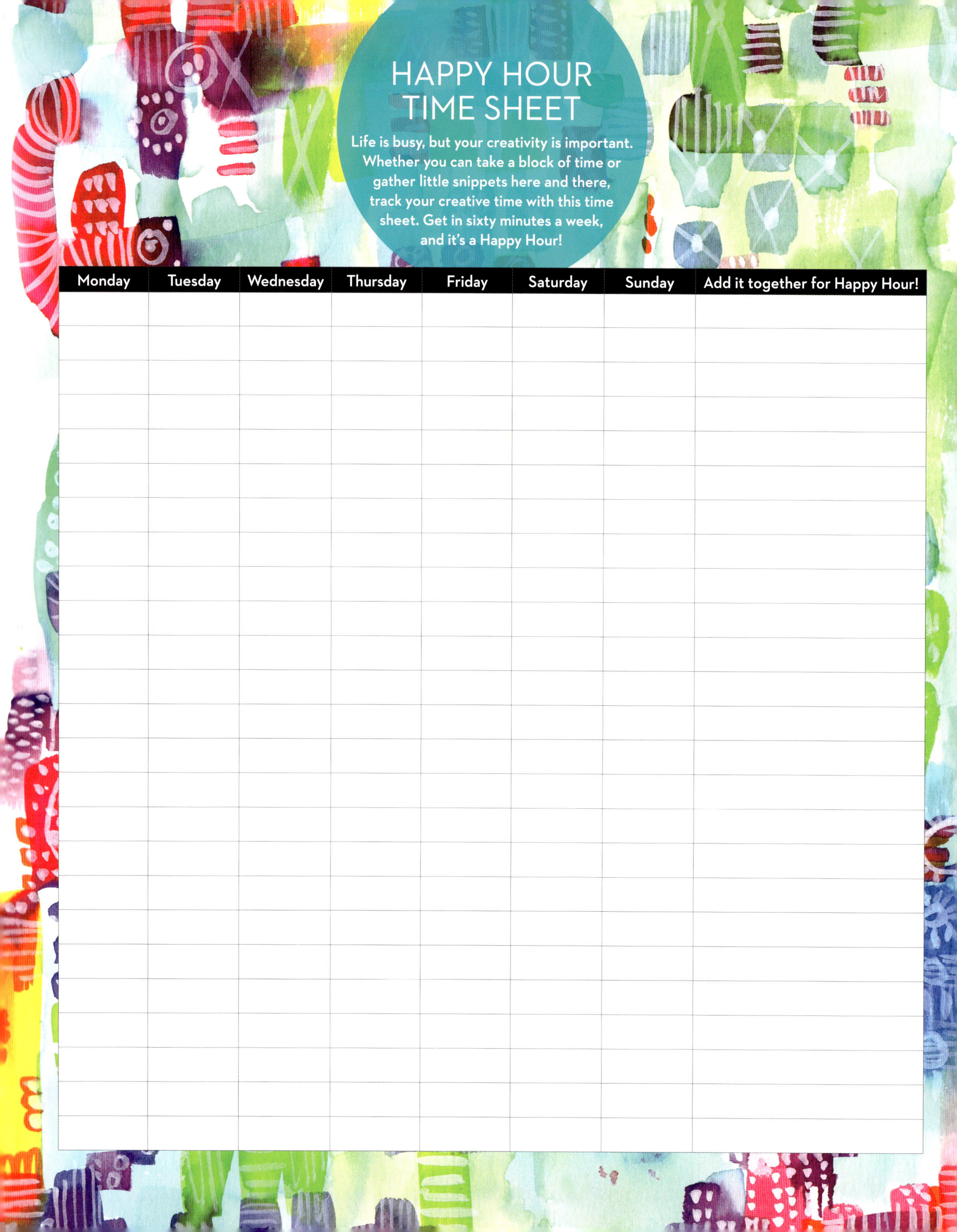

HAPPY HOUR TIME SHEET

Life is busy, but your creativity is important. Whether you can take a block of time or gather little snippets here and there, track your creative time with this time sheet. Get in sixty minutes a week, and it's a Happy Hour!

Monday	Tuesday	Wednesday	Thursday	Friday	Saturday	Sunday	Add it together for Happy Hour!

Whimsical

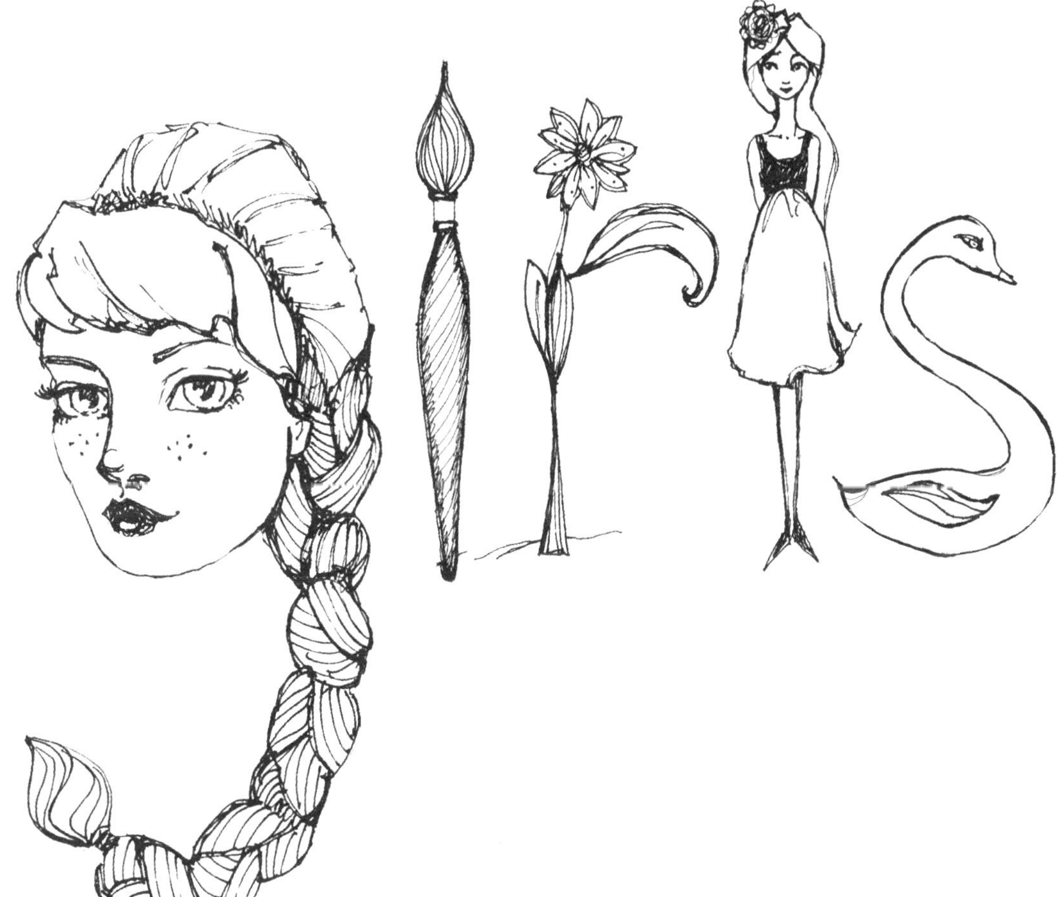

girls

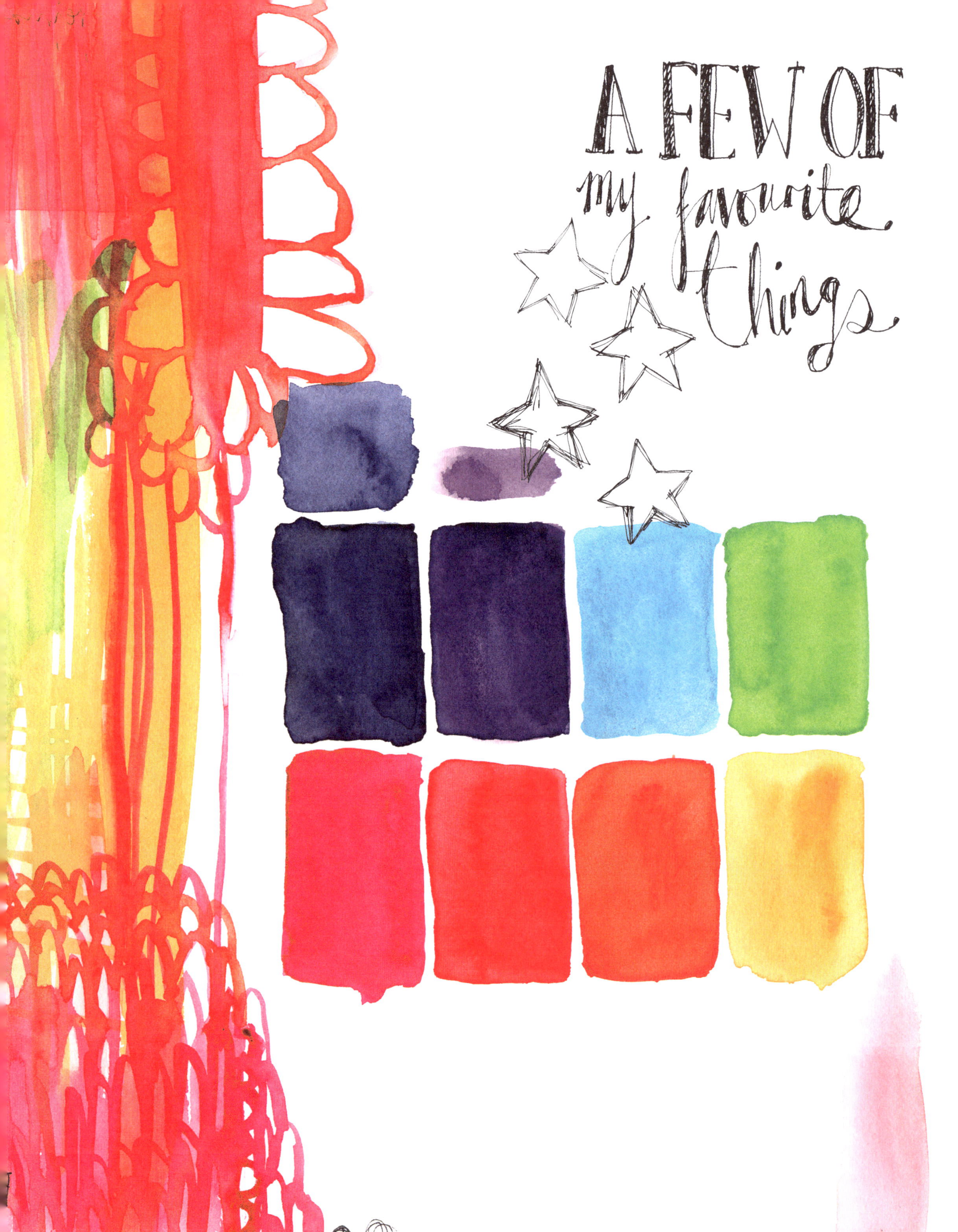

A FEW OF
my favourite
things

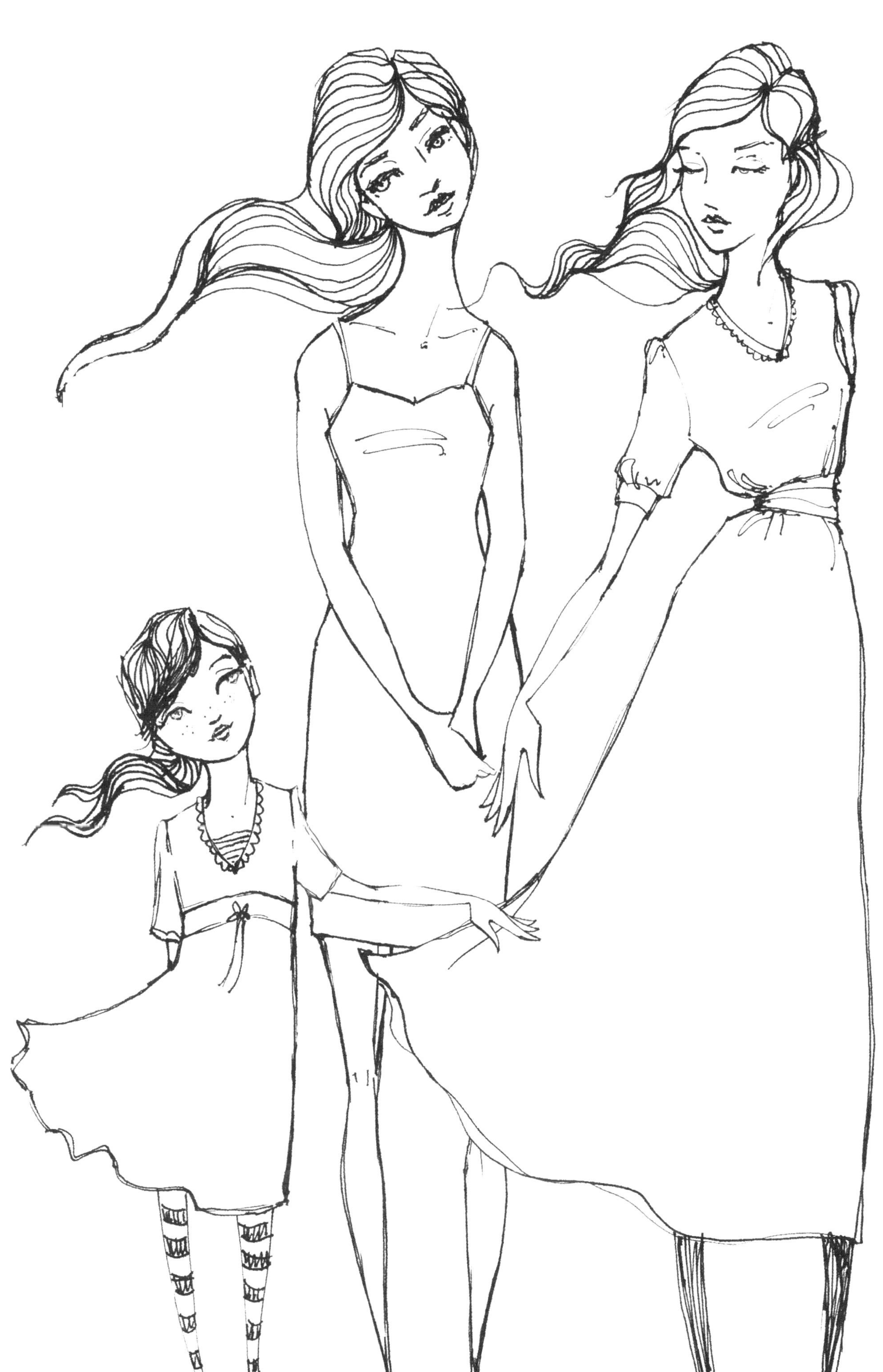

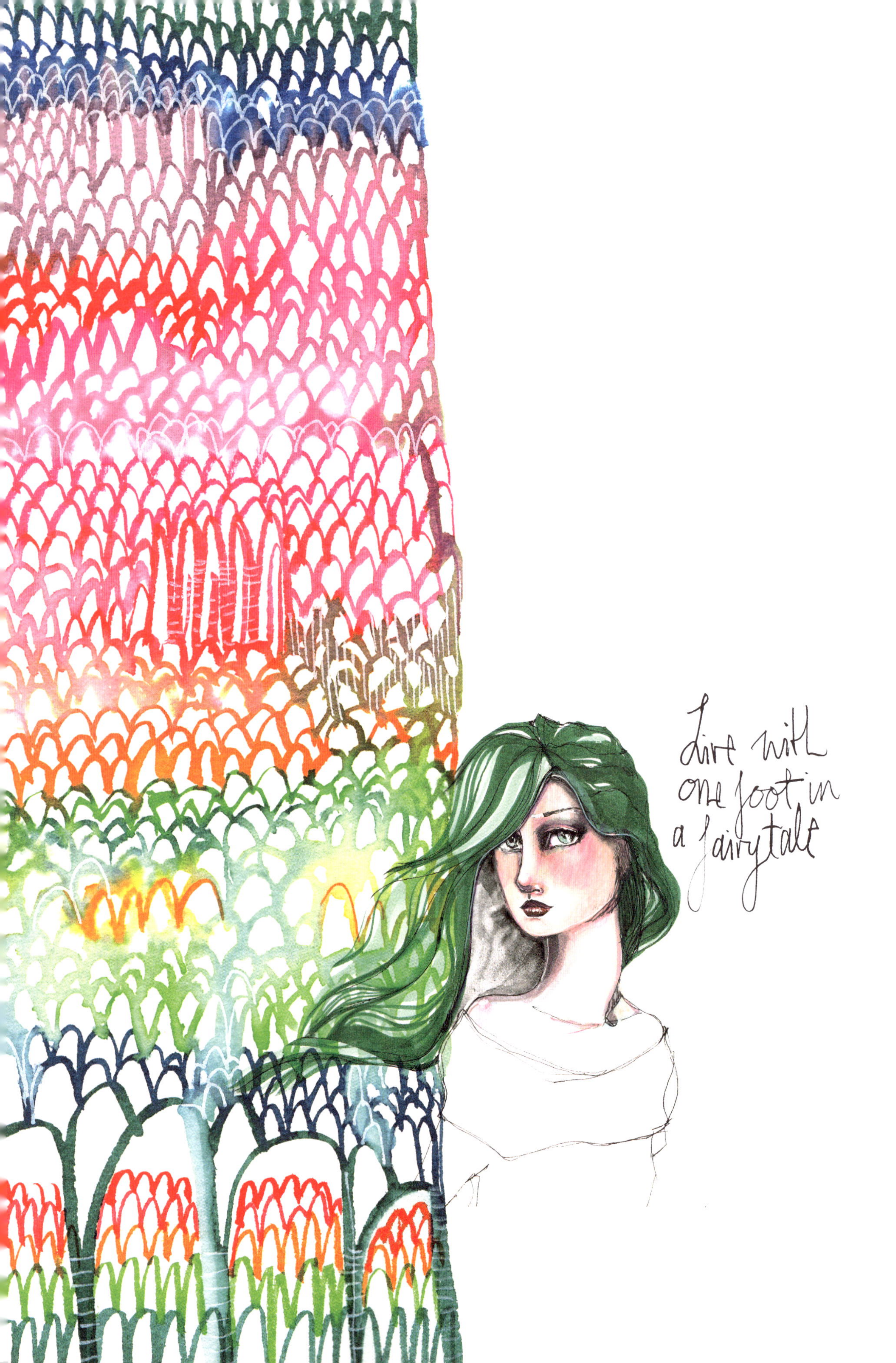
Live with
one foot in
a fairytale

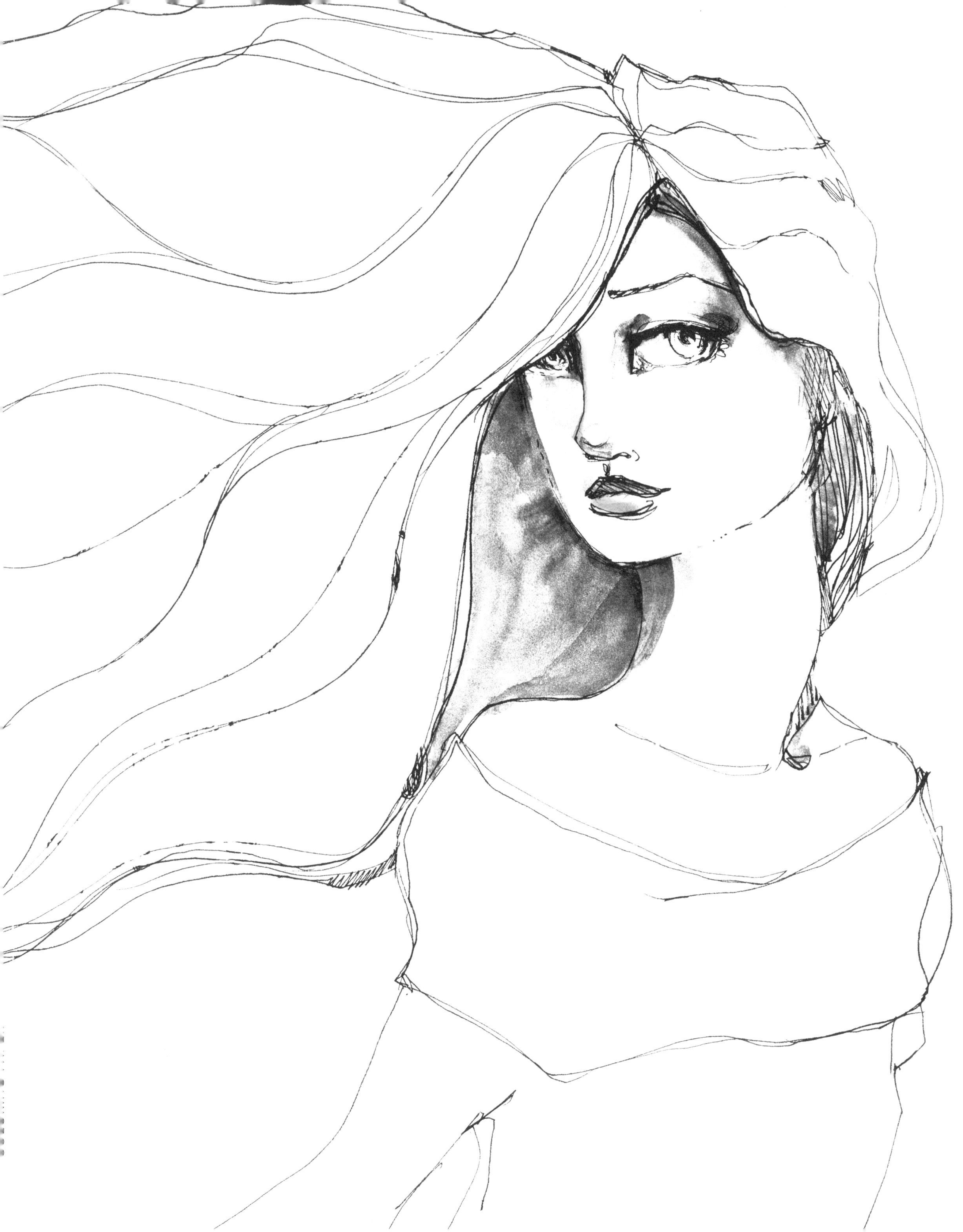

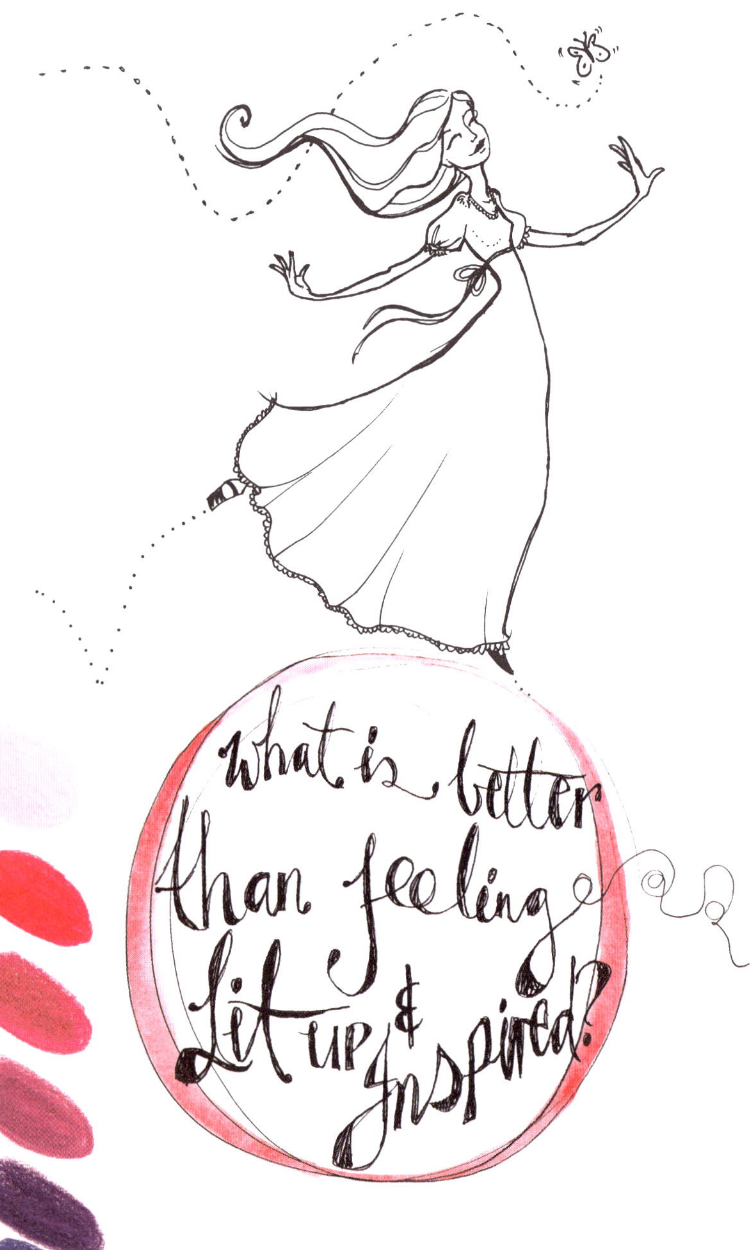

what is better than feeling lit up & inspired?

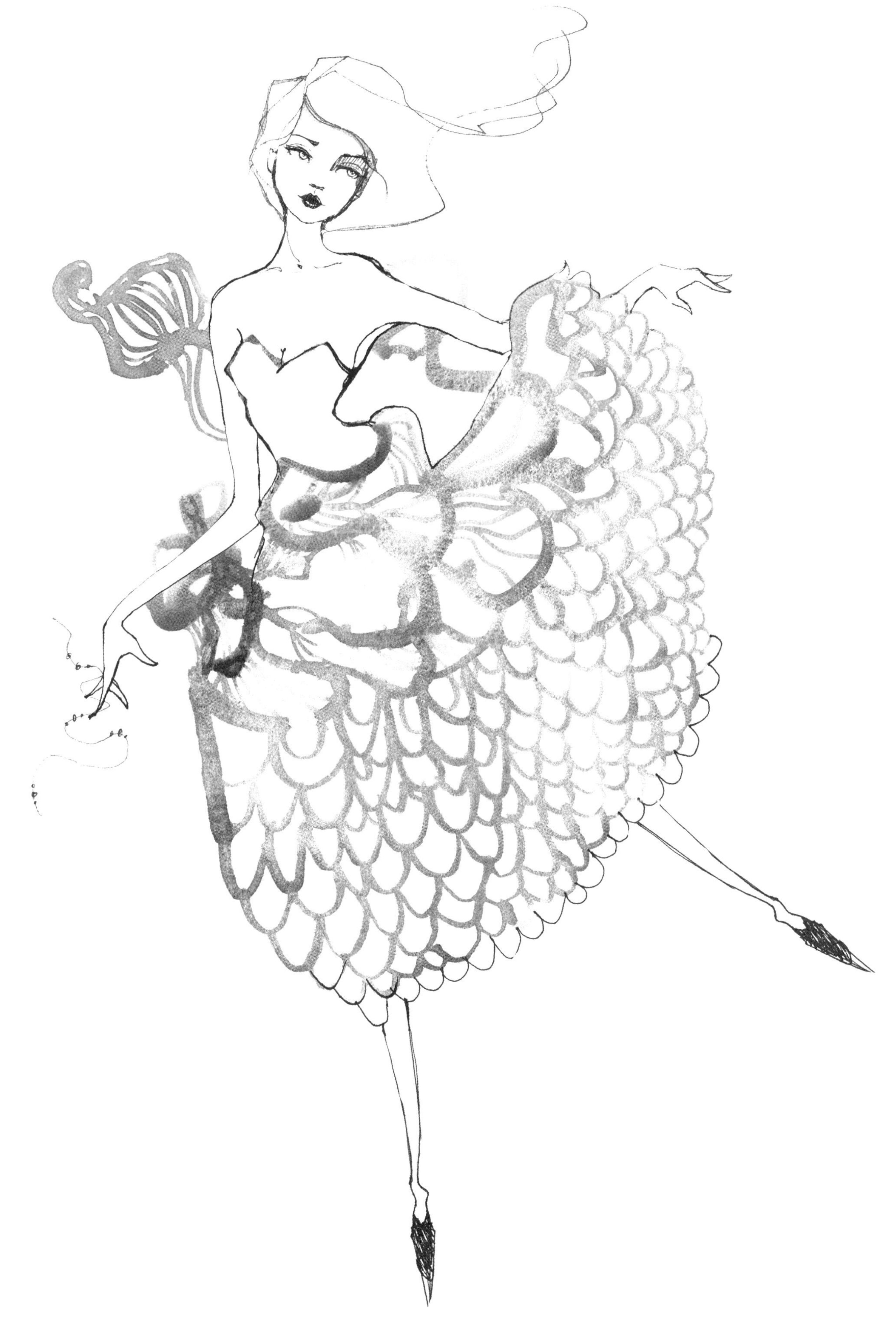

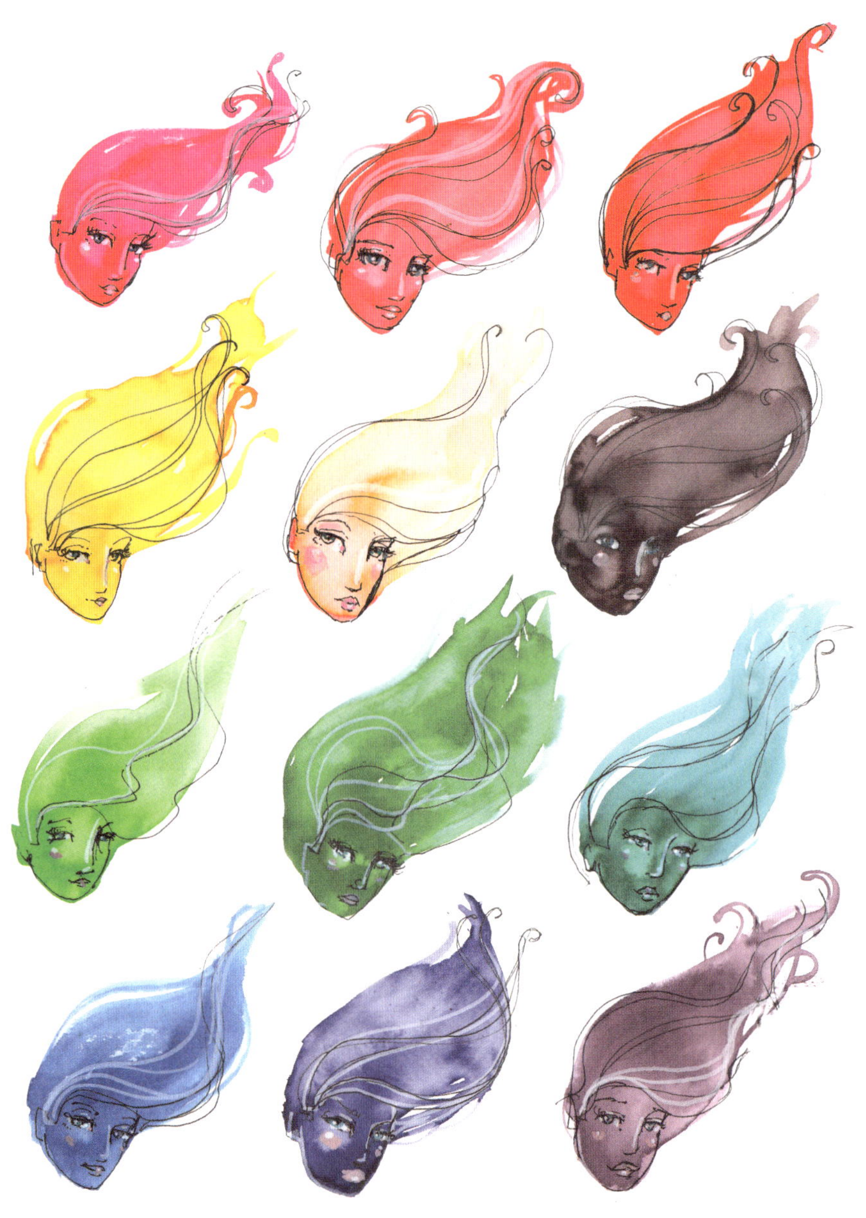

DRAW OUT
your wonder

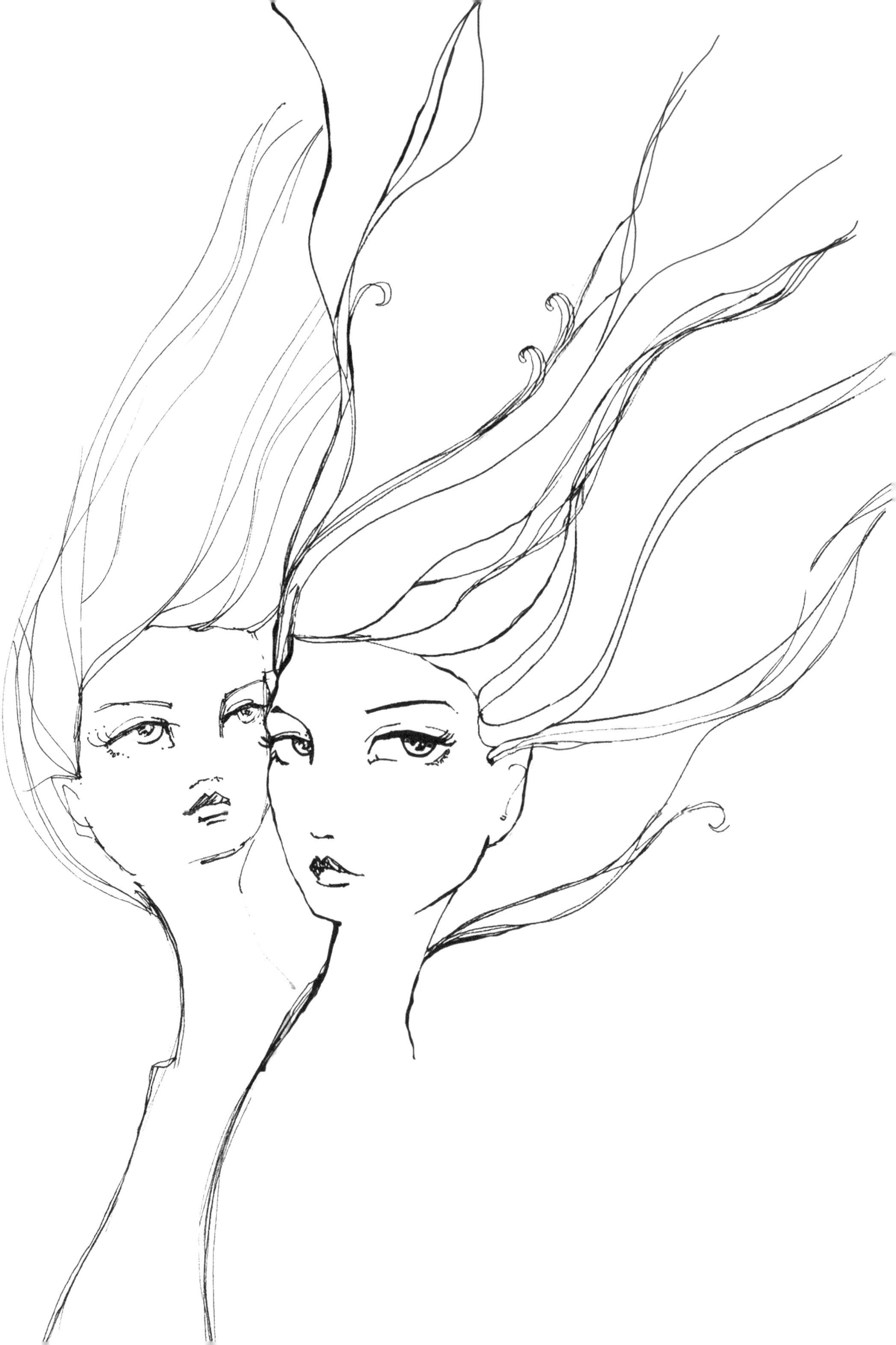

COLORING PAPER

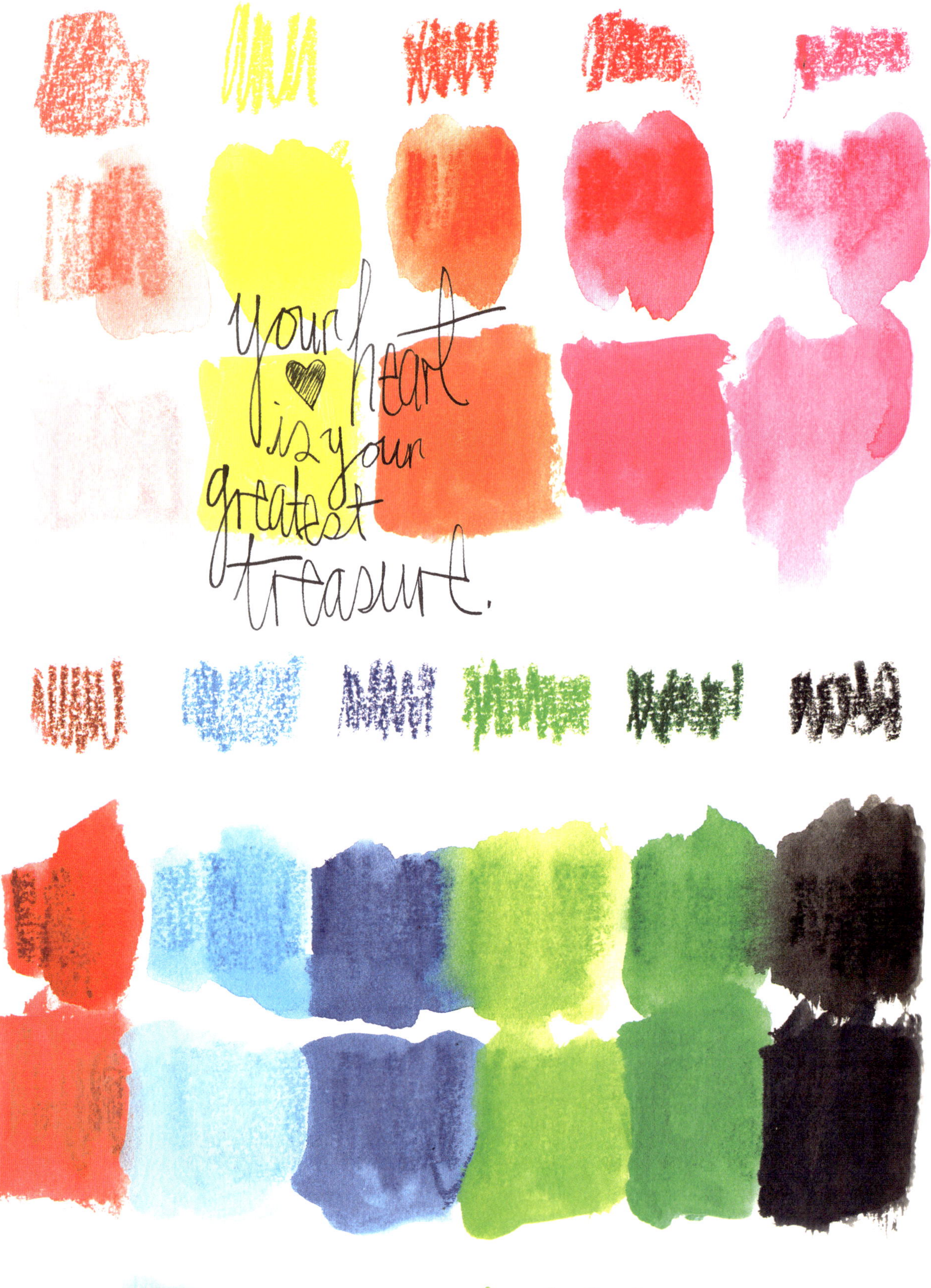

your heart
is your
greatest
treasure.

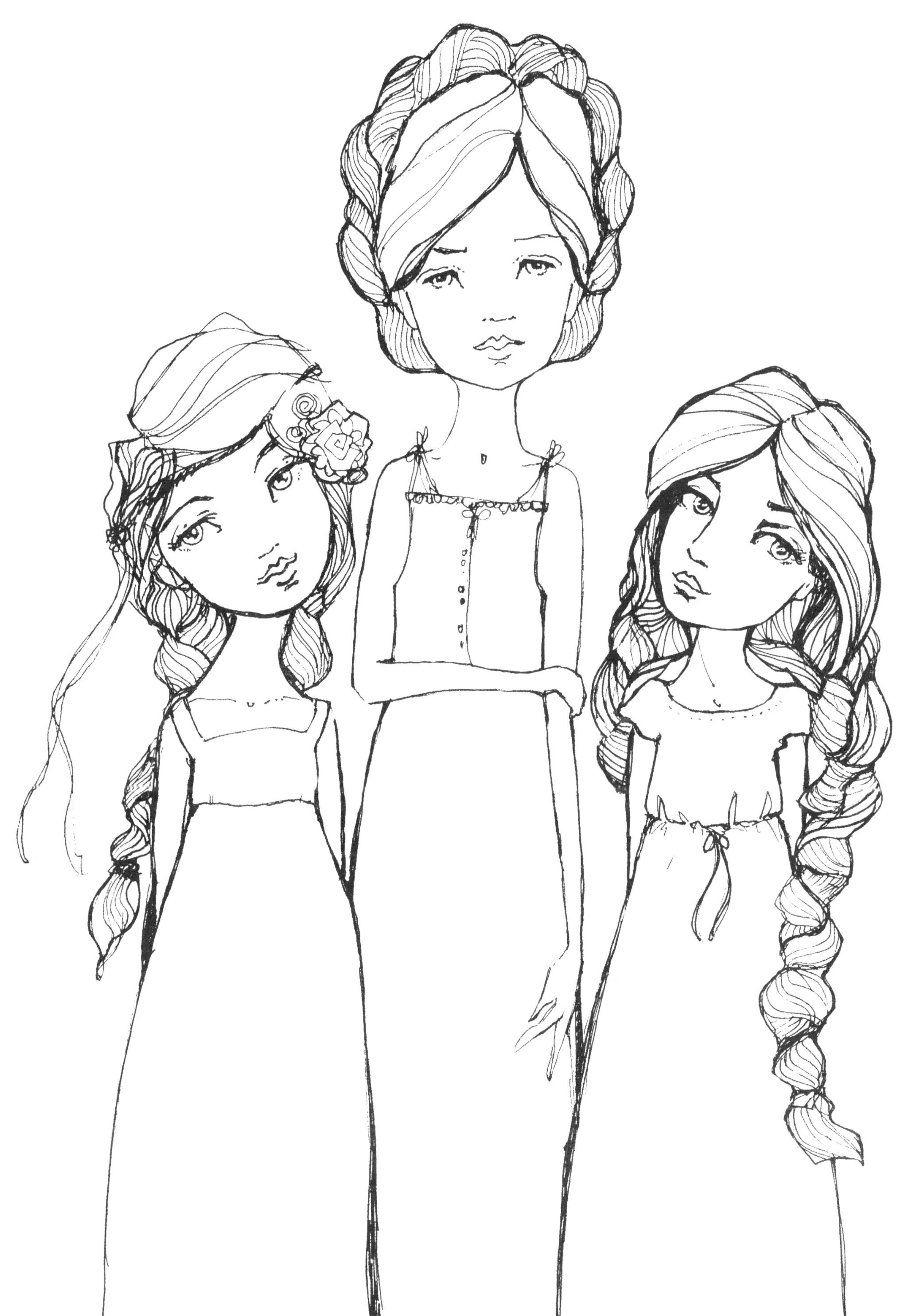

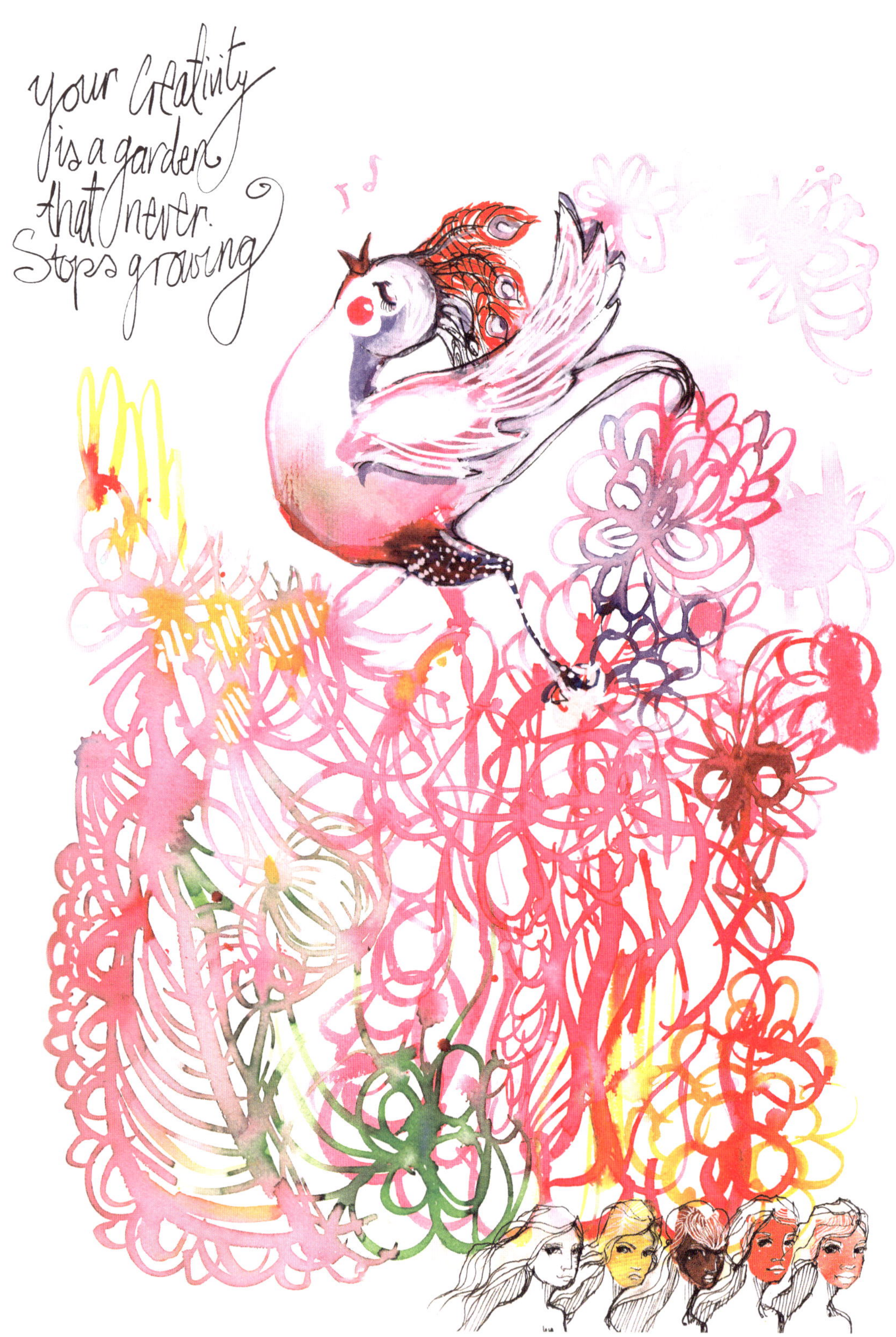

your creativity
is a garden
that never
stops growing

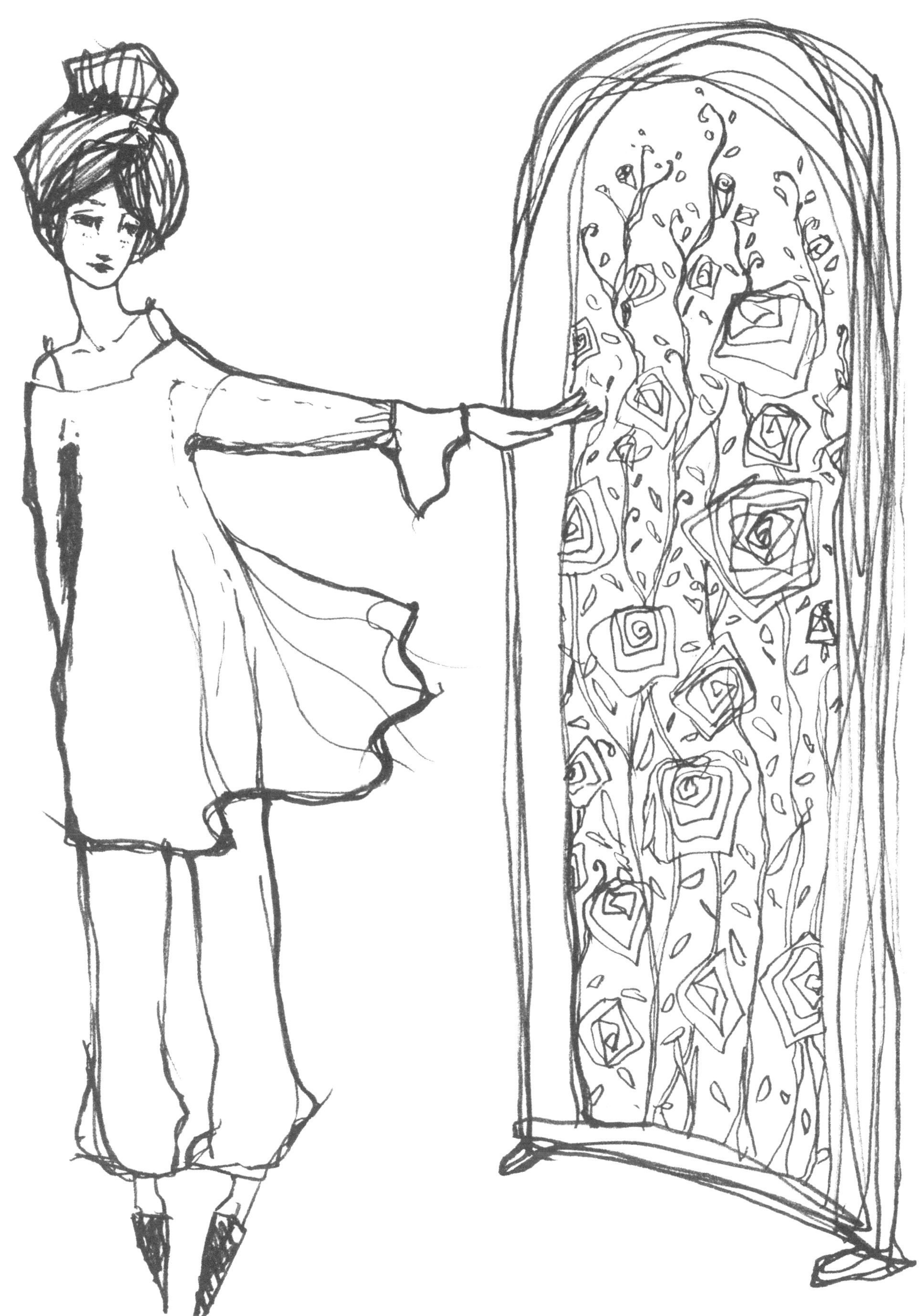

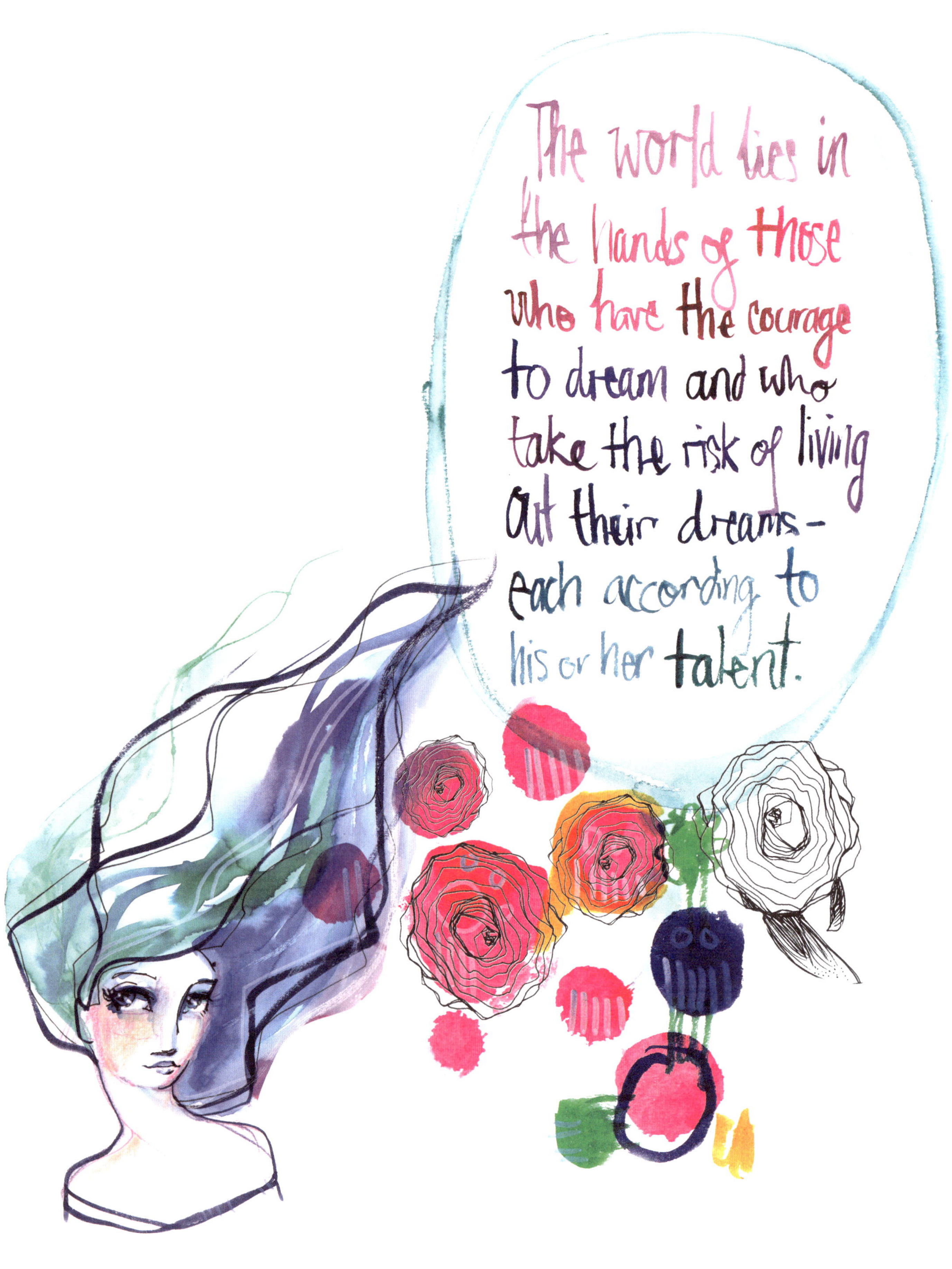
The world lies in the hands of those who have the courage to dream and who take the risk of living out their dreams - each according to his or her talent.

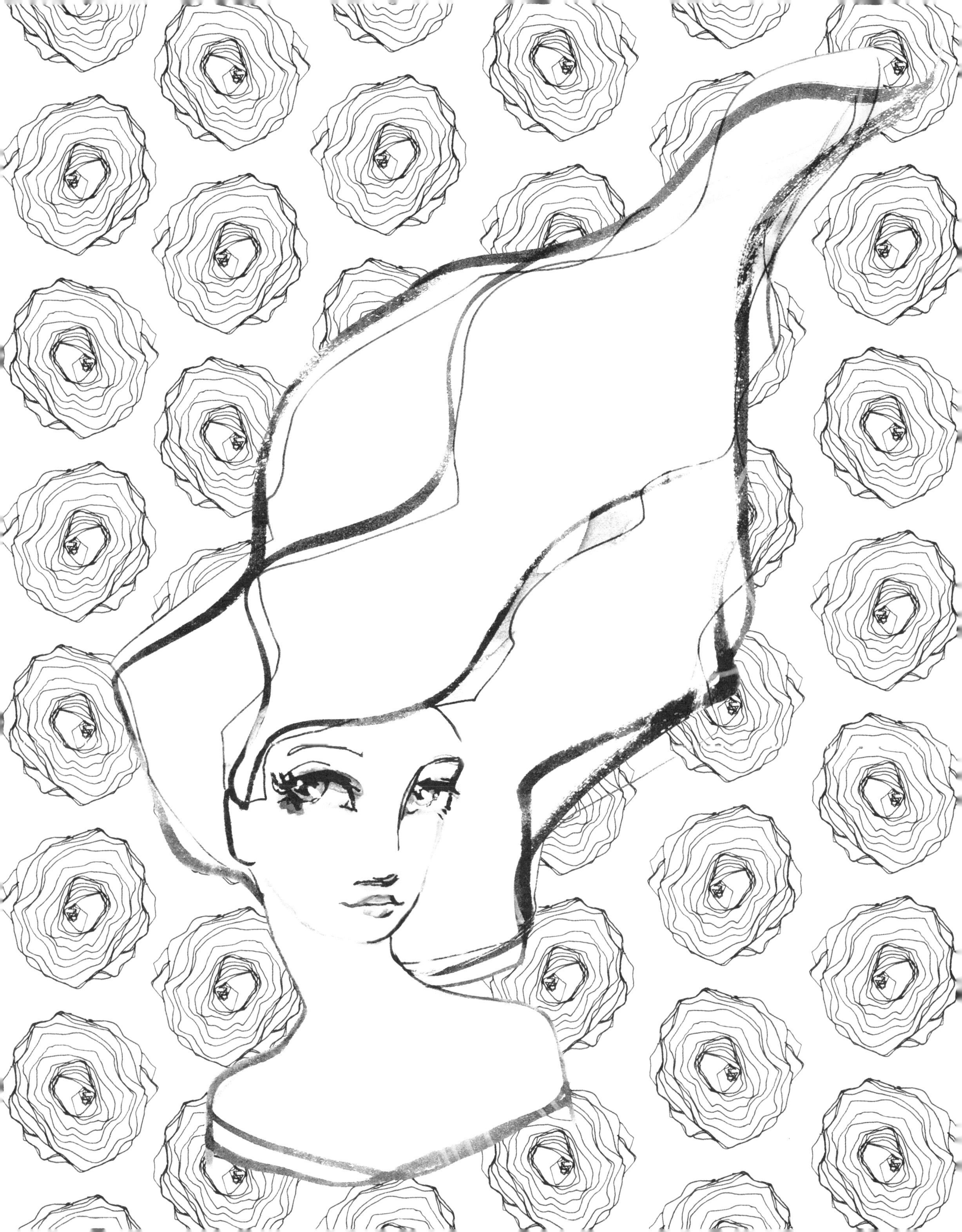

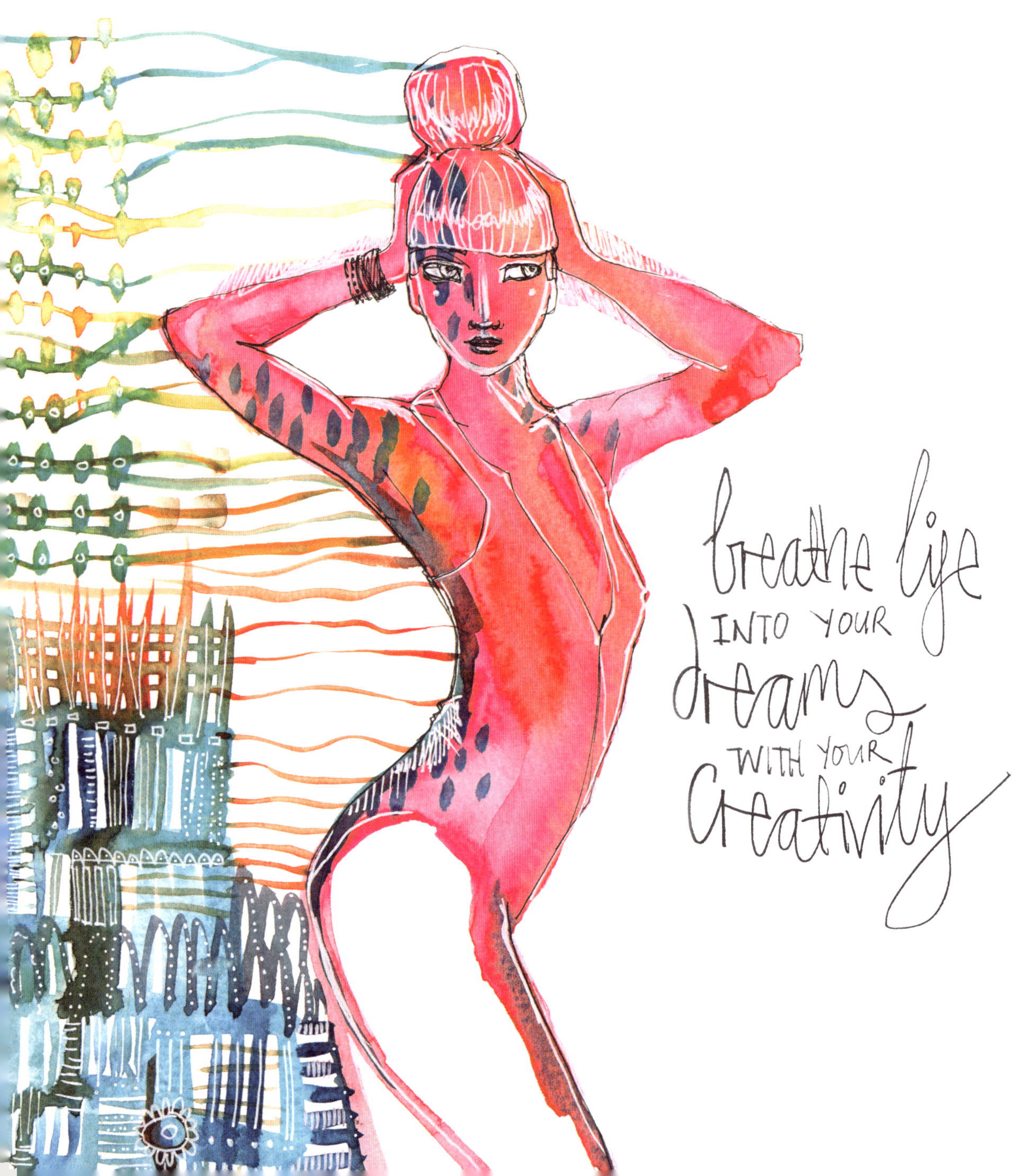
breathe life
INTO YOUR
dreams
WITH YOUR
creativity

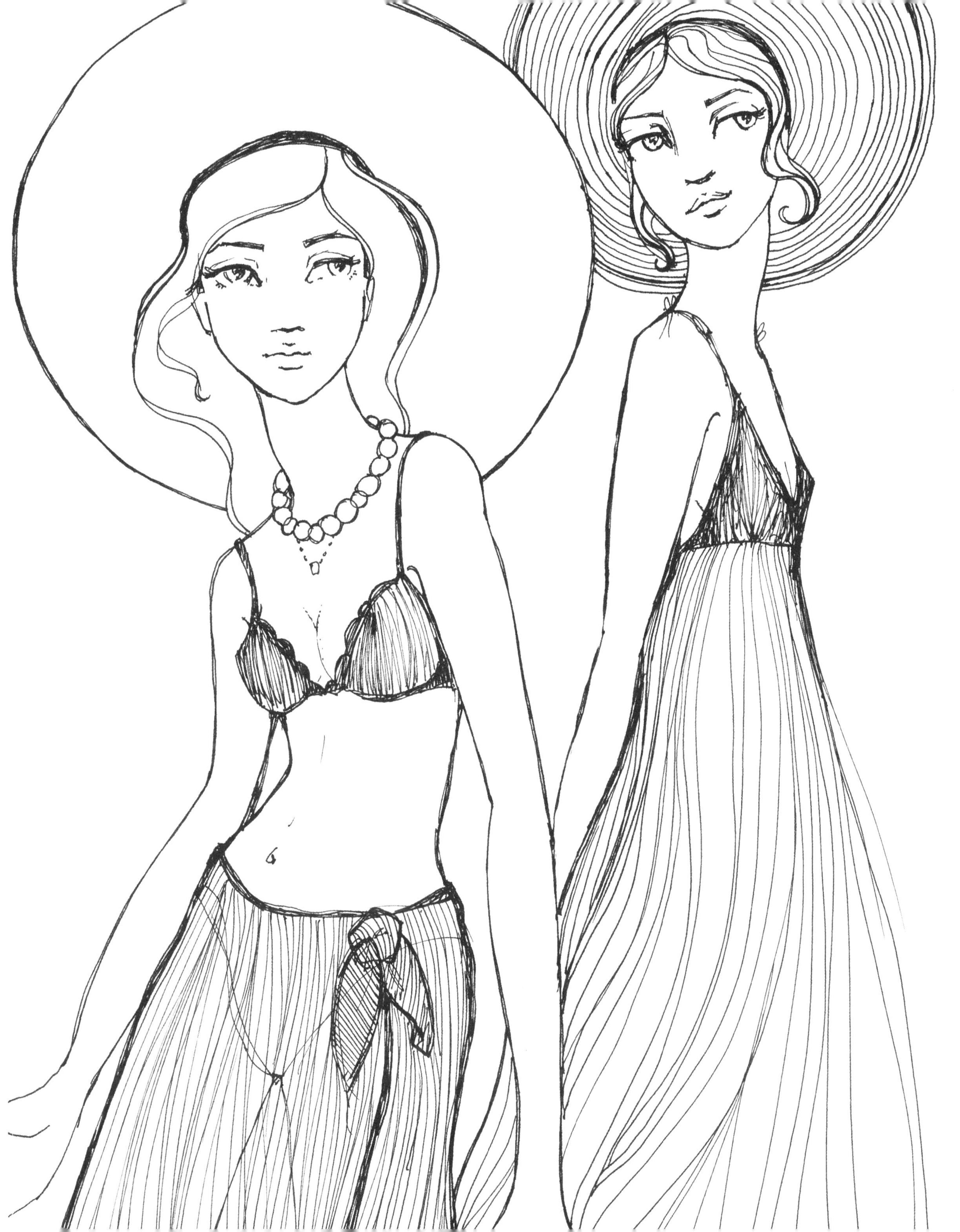

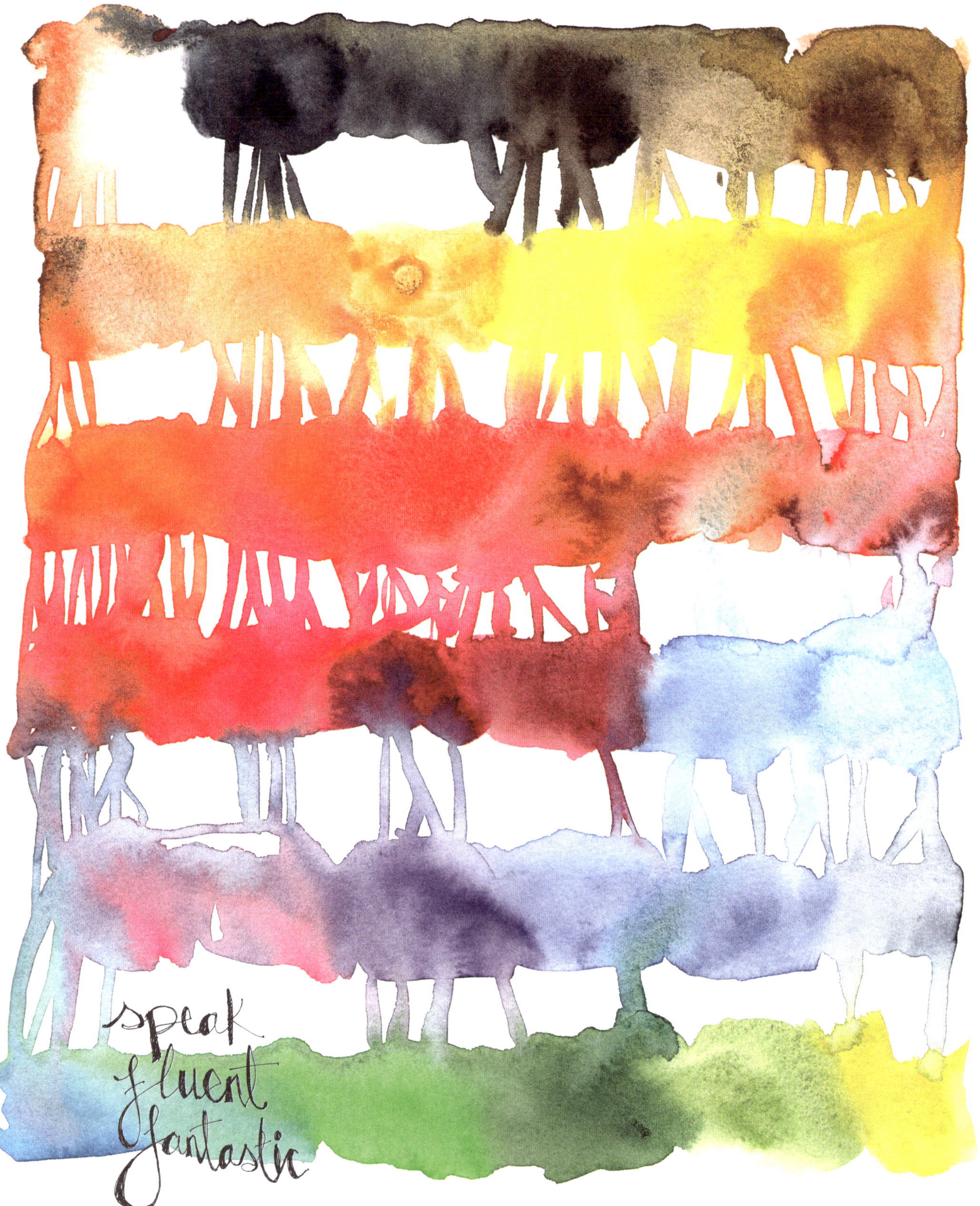

speak
fluent
fantastic

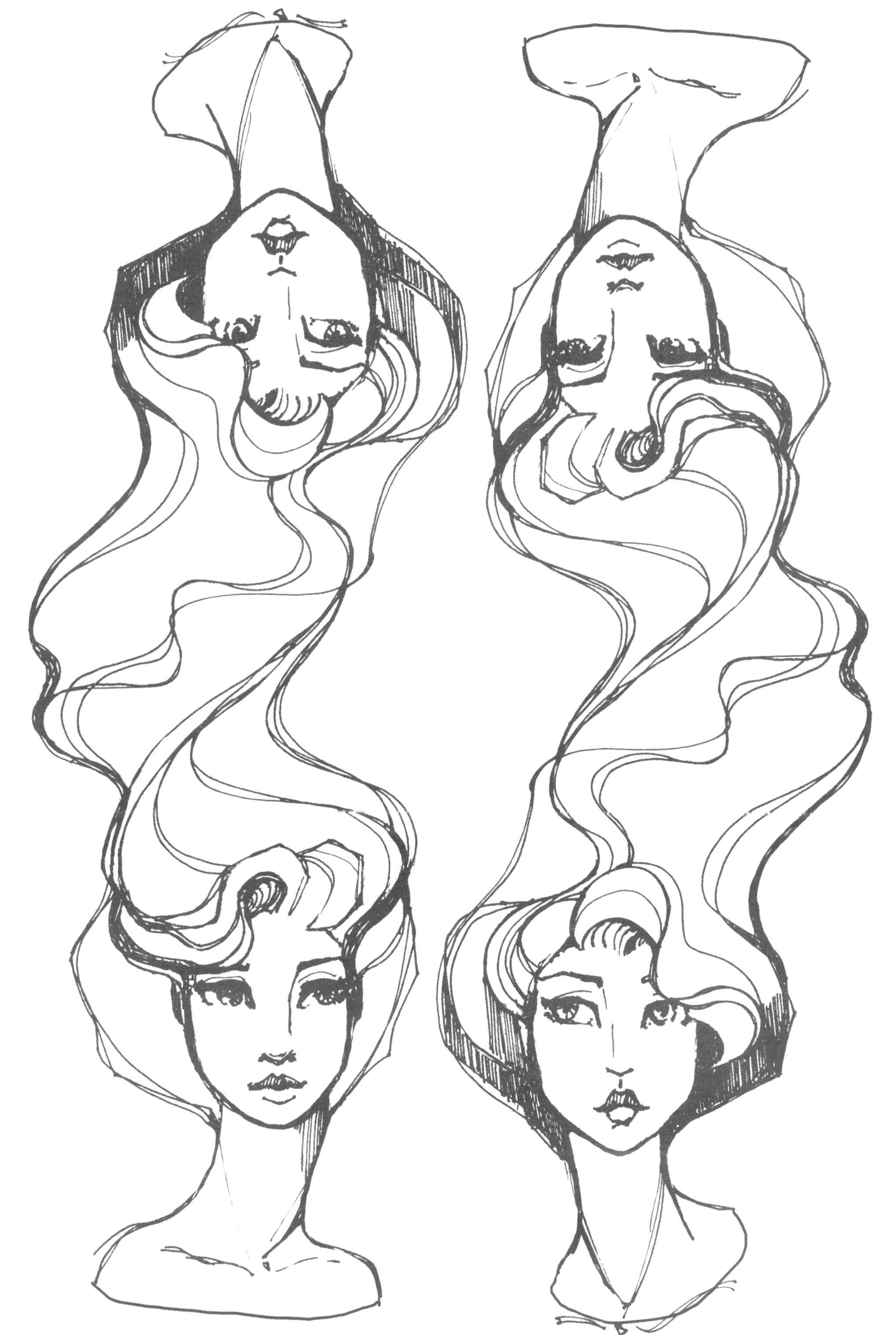

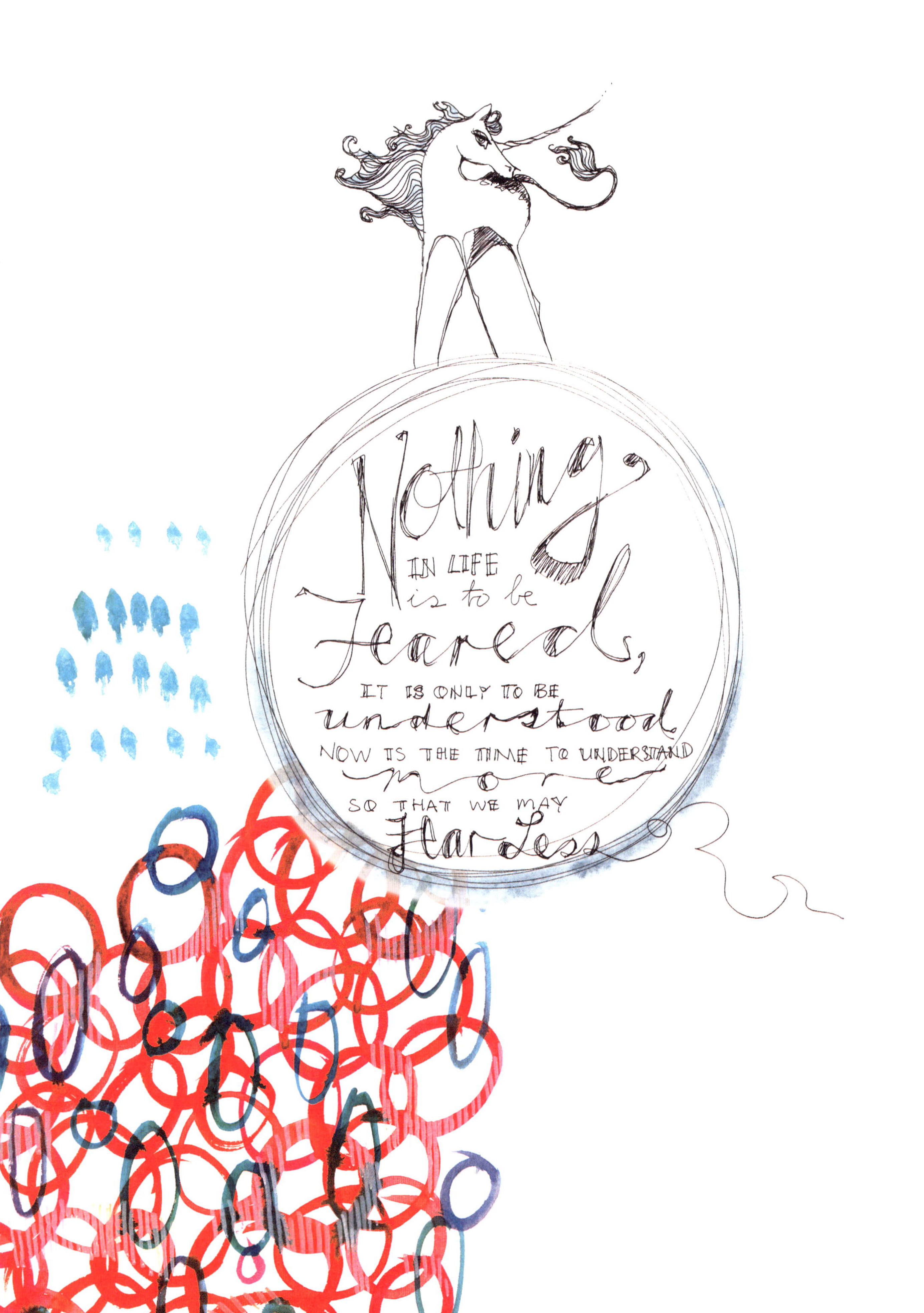
Nothing
IN LIFE
is to be
Feared,
IT IS ONLY TO BE
understood.
NOW IS THE TIME TO UNDERSTAND
more
SO THAT WE MAY
Fear Less

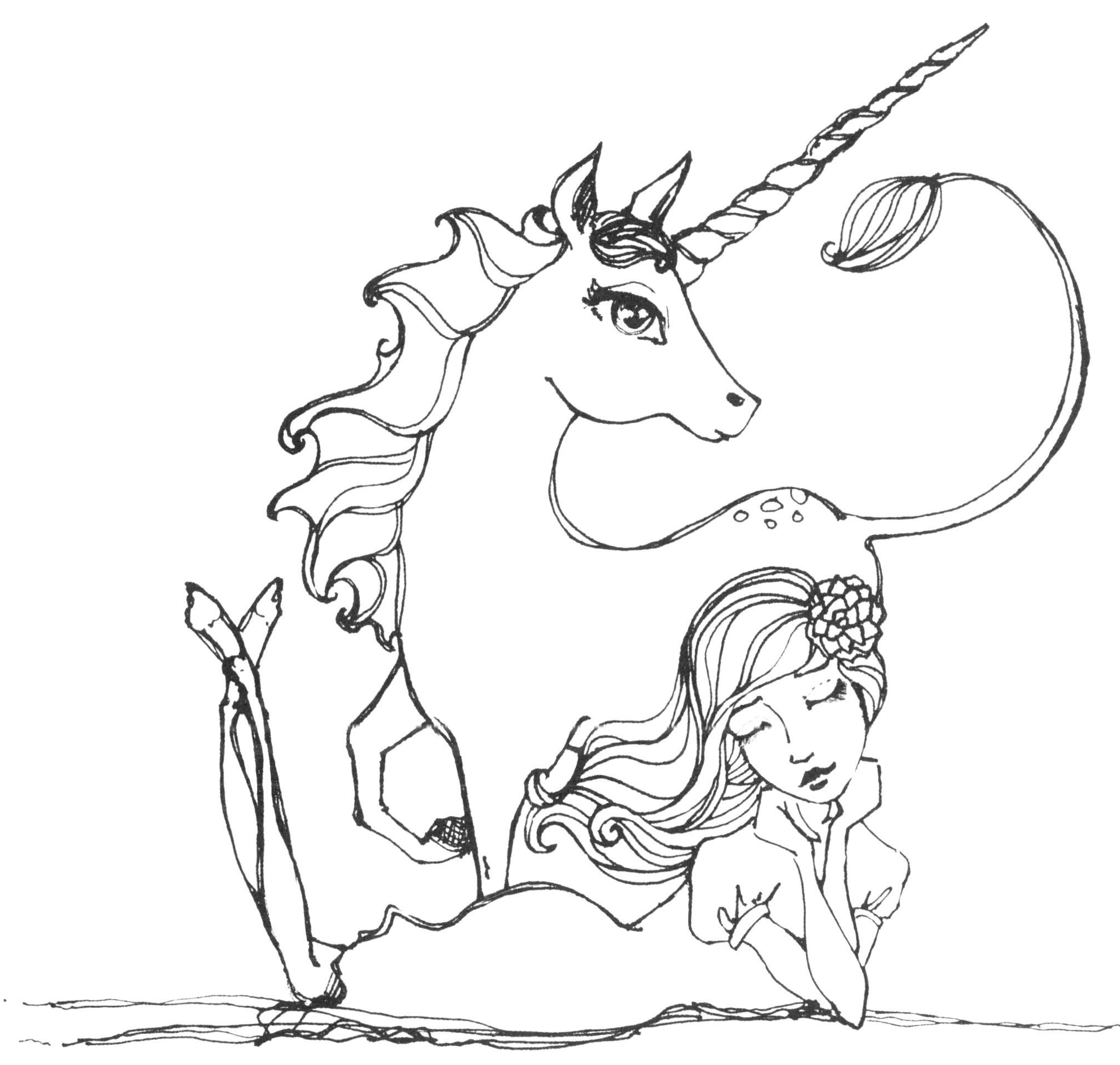

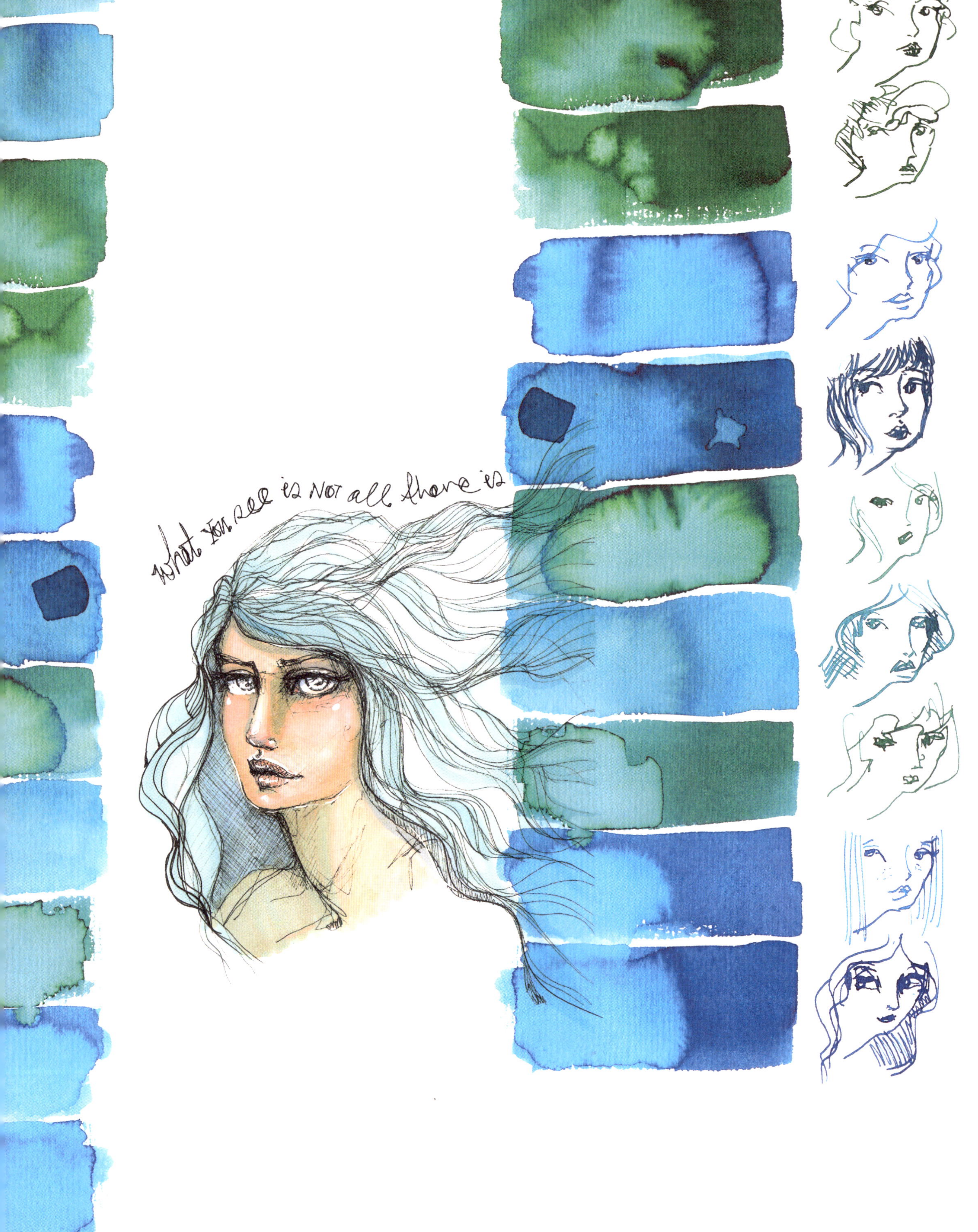

what you see is not all there is

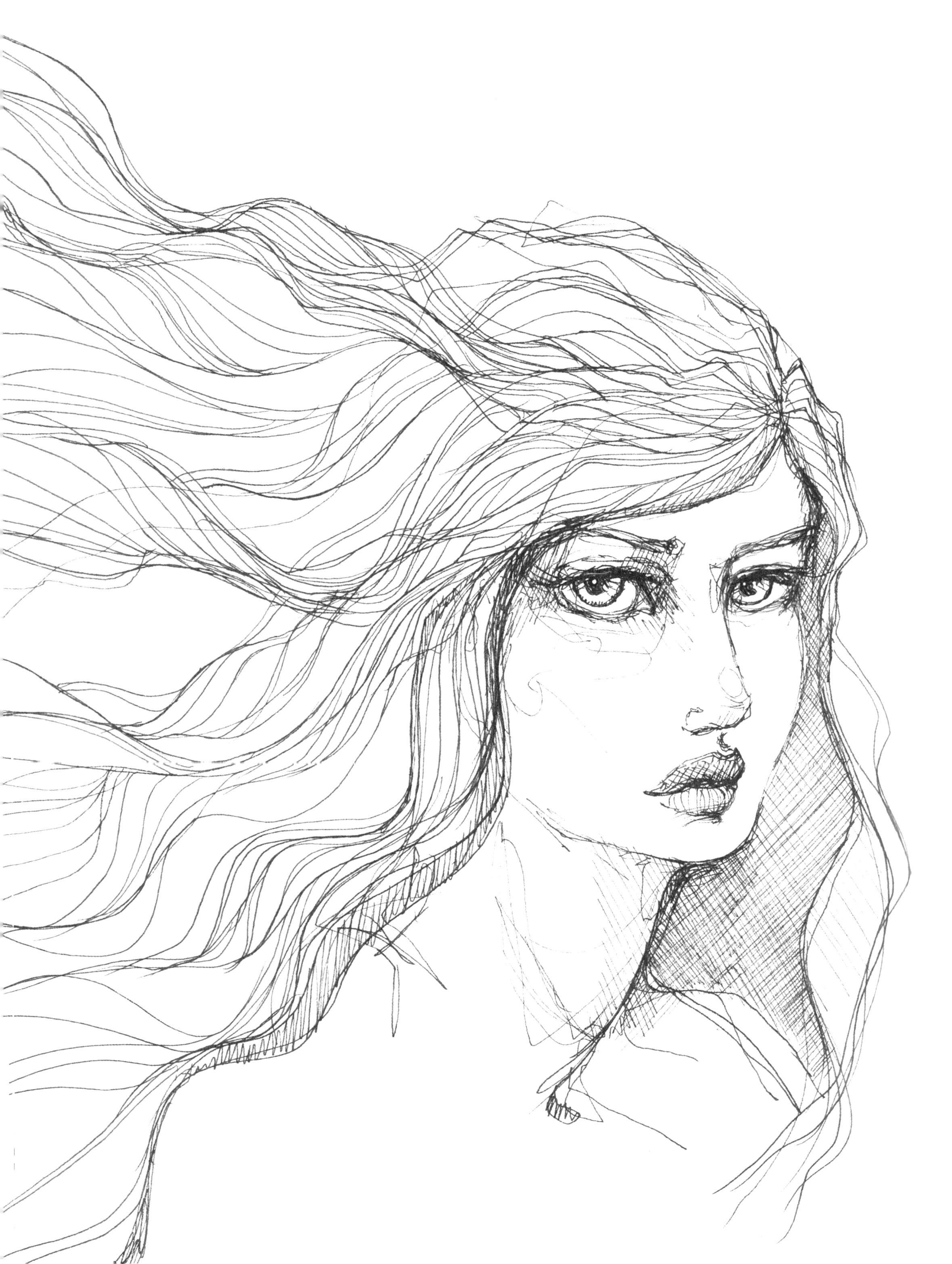

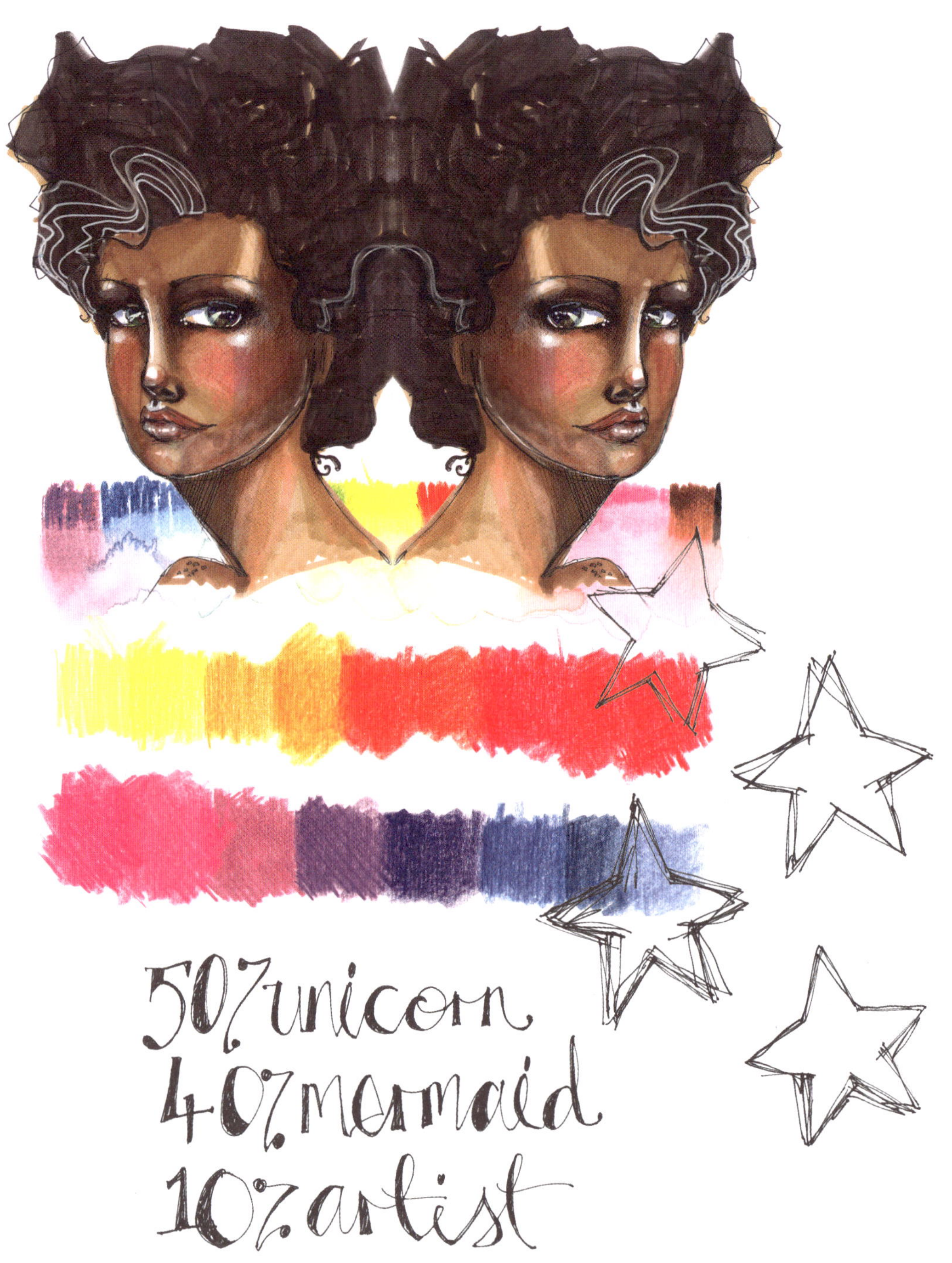

50% unicorn
40% mermaid
10% artist

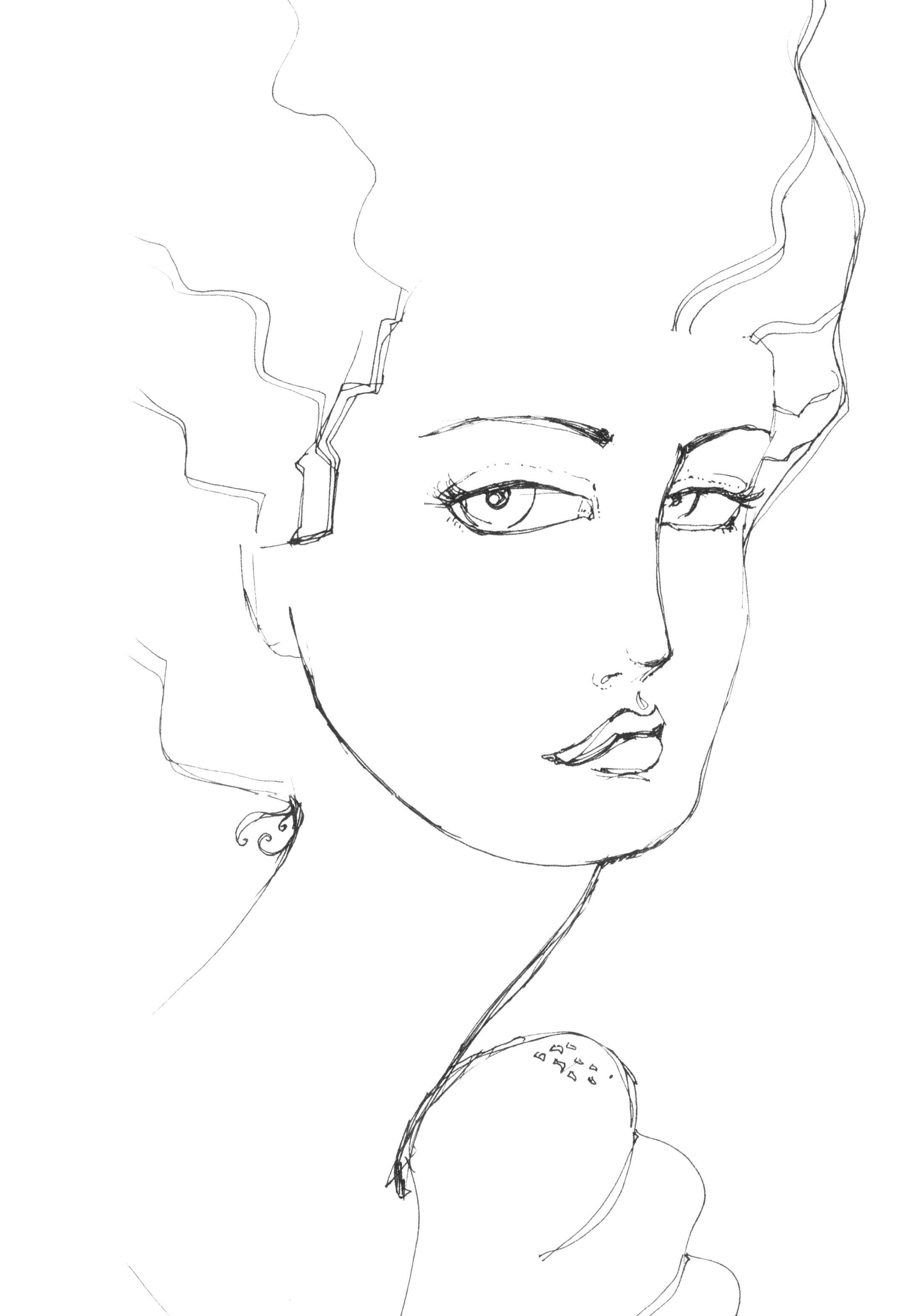

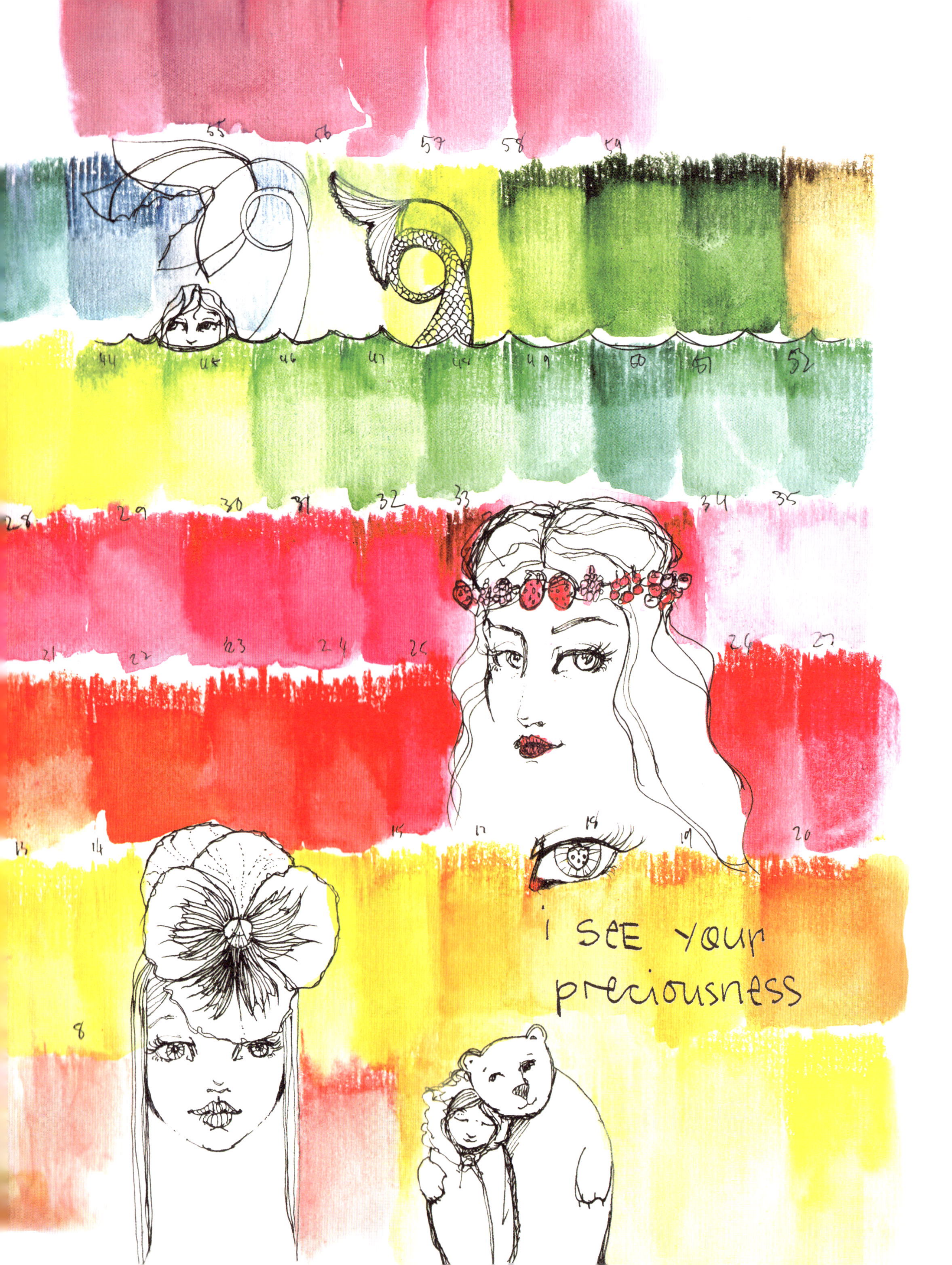
i see your
preciousness

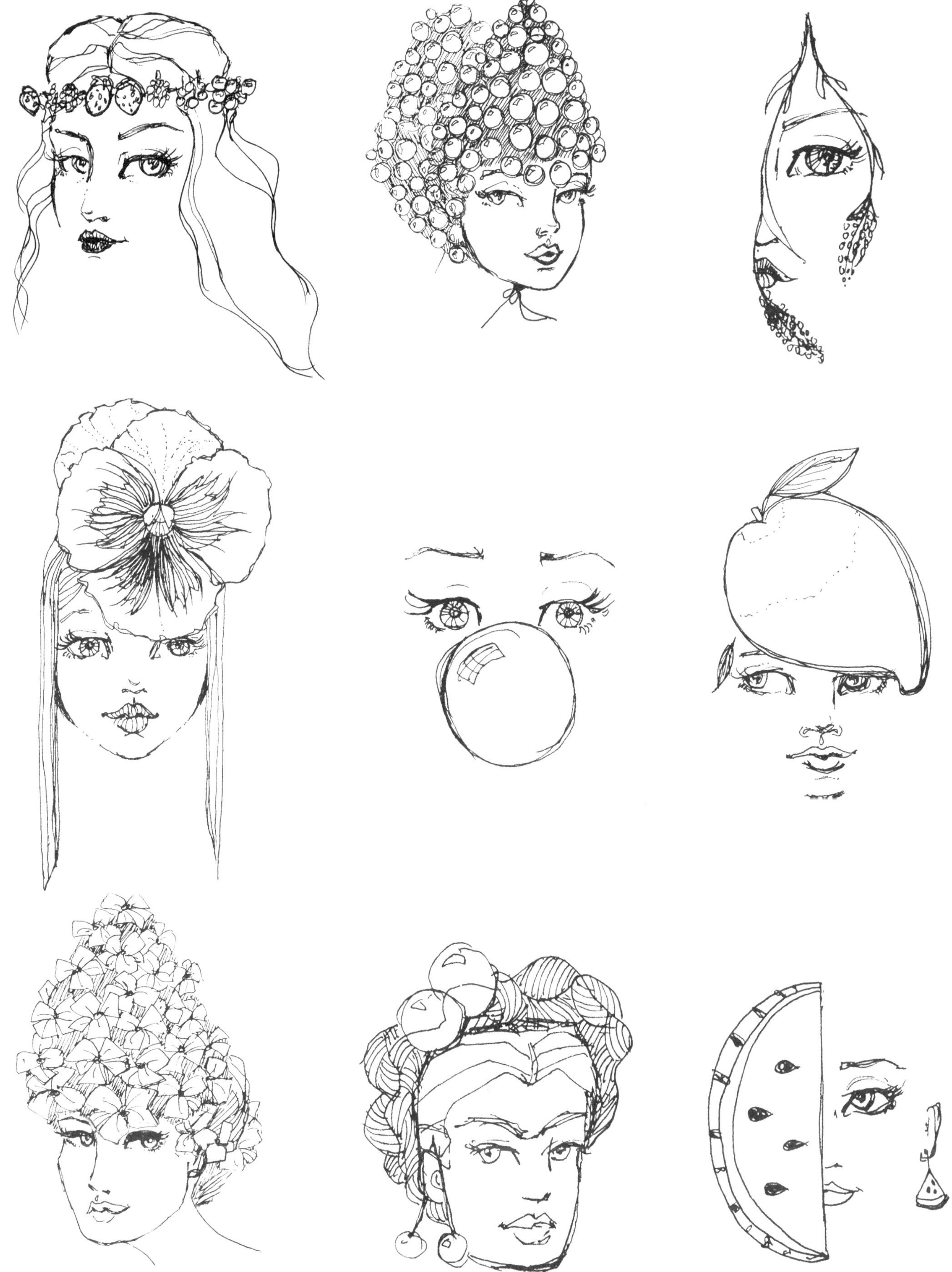

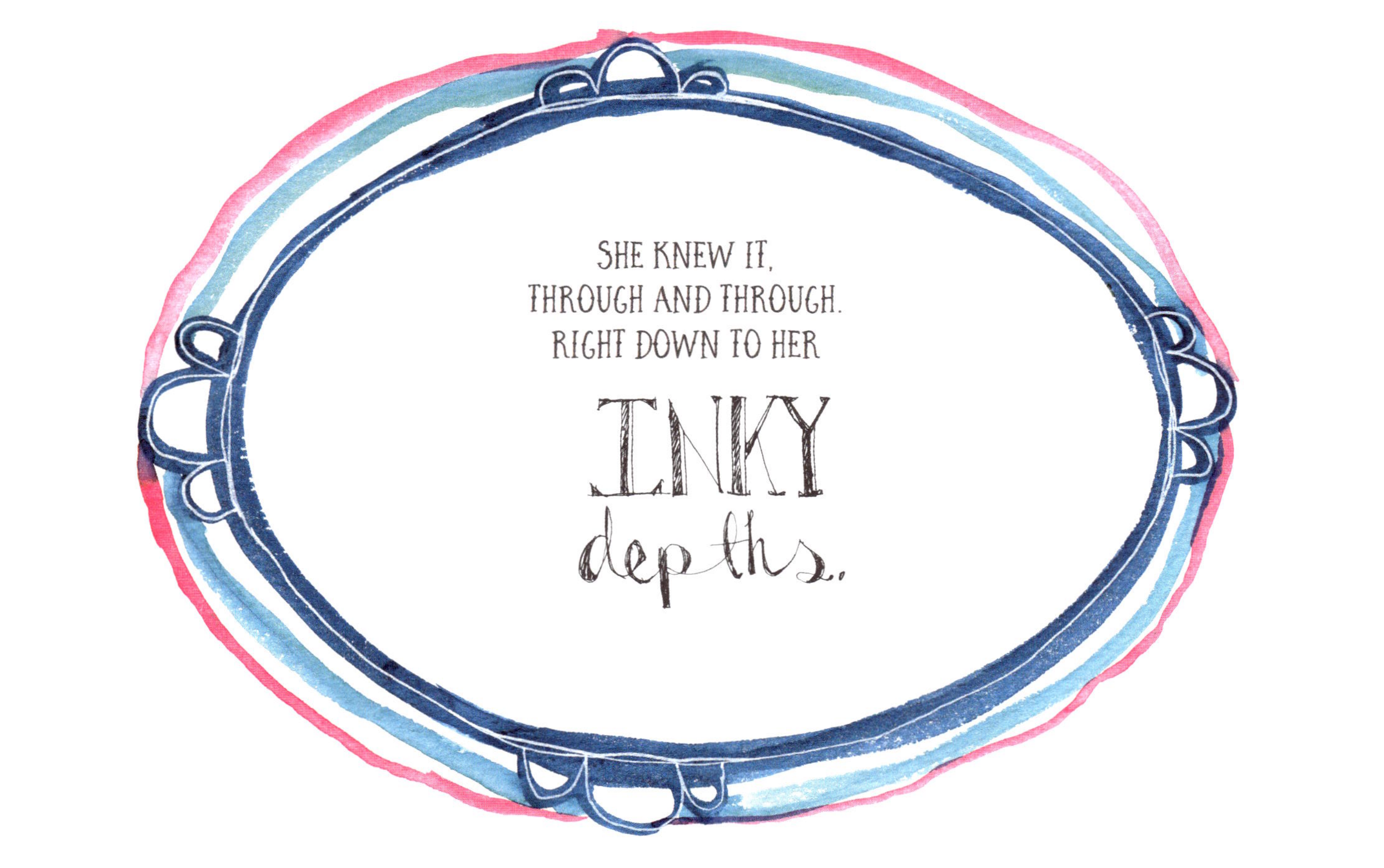

SHE KNEW IT,
THROUGH AND THROUGH.
RIGHT DOWN TO HER
INKY
depths.

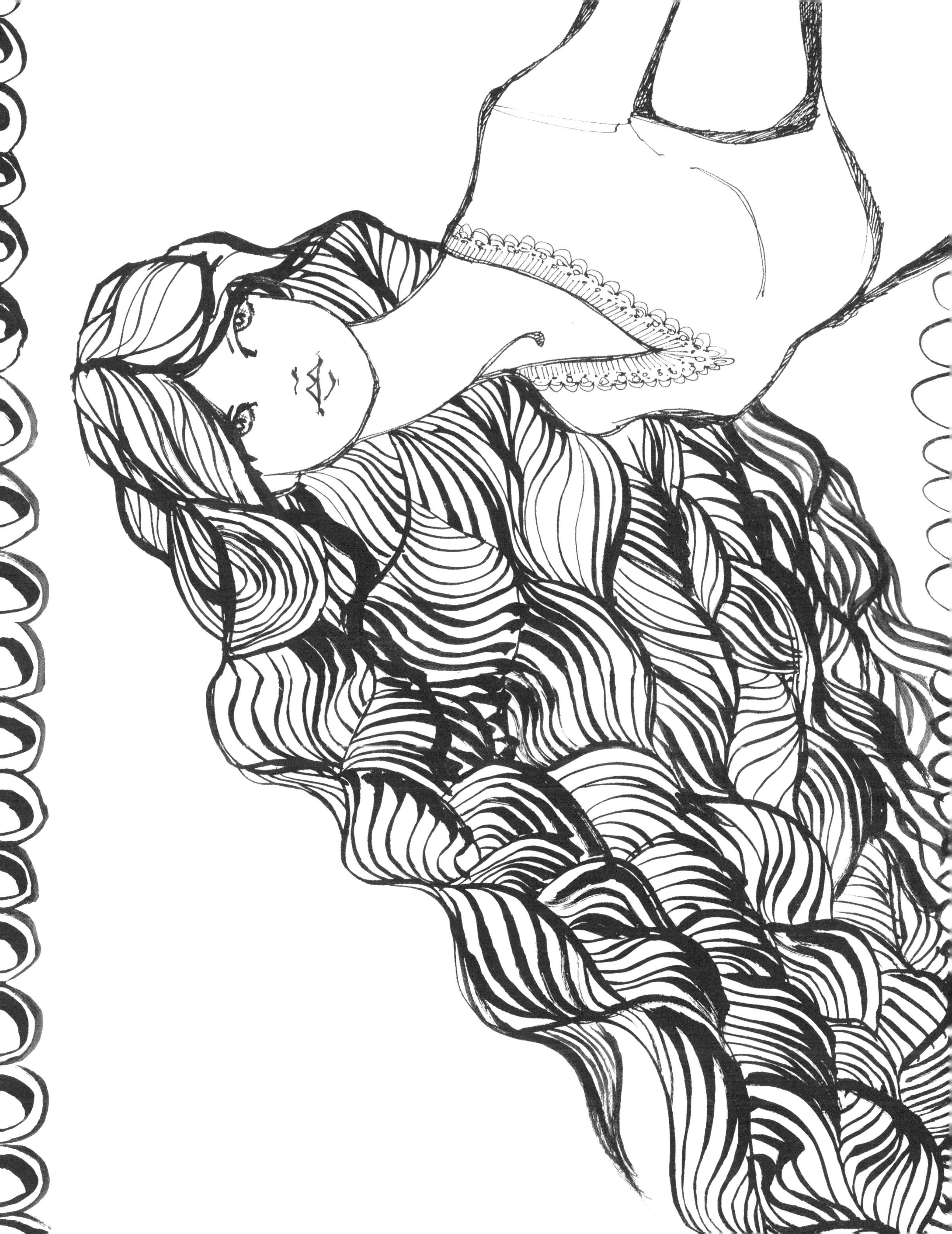

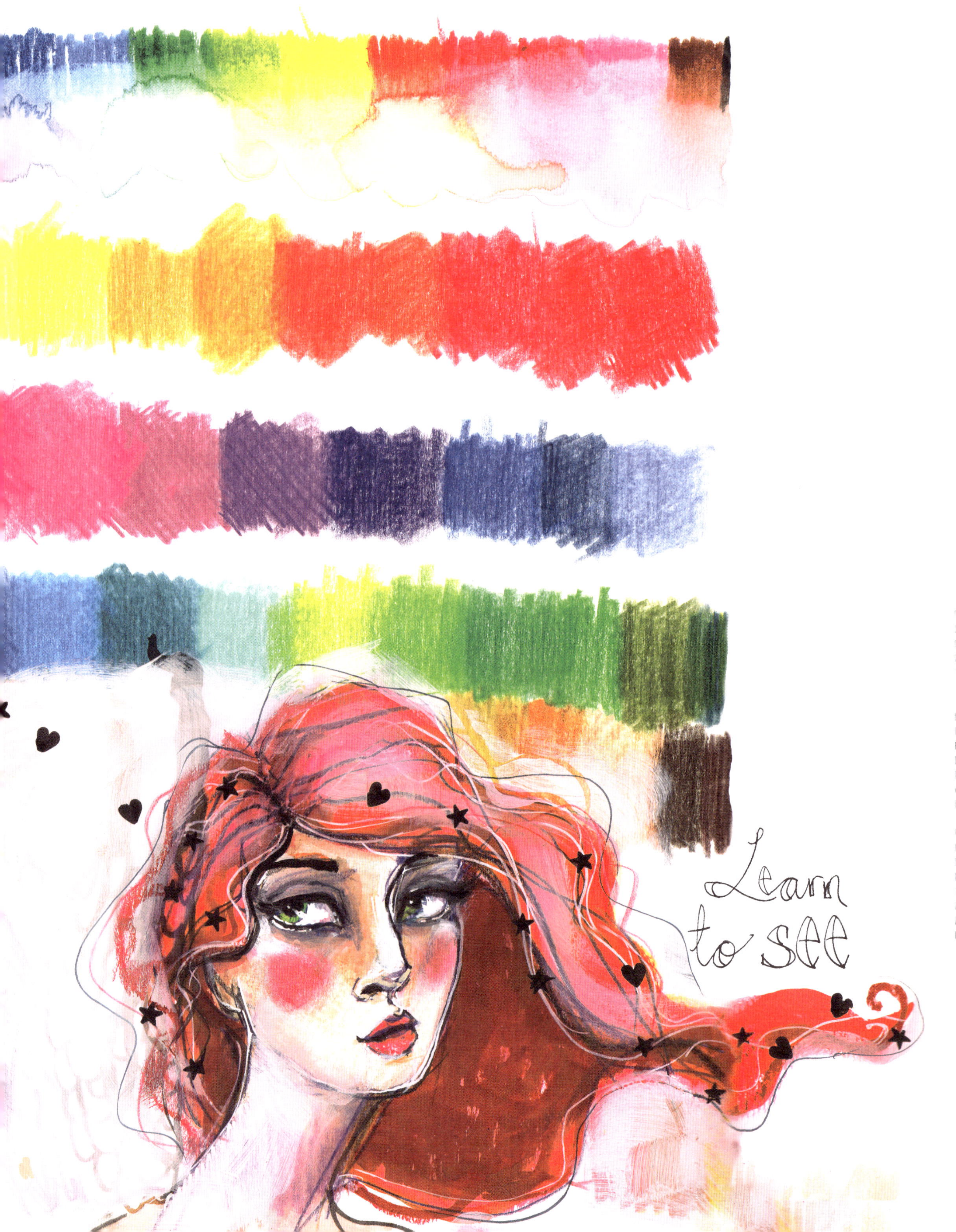
Learn
to see

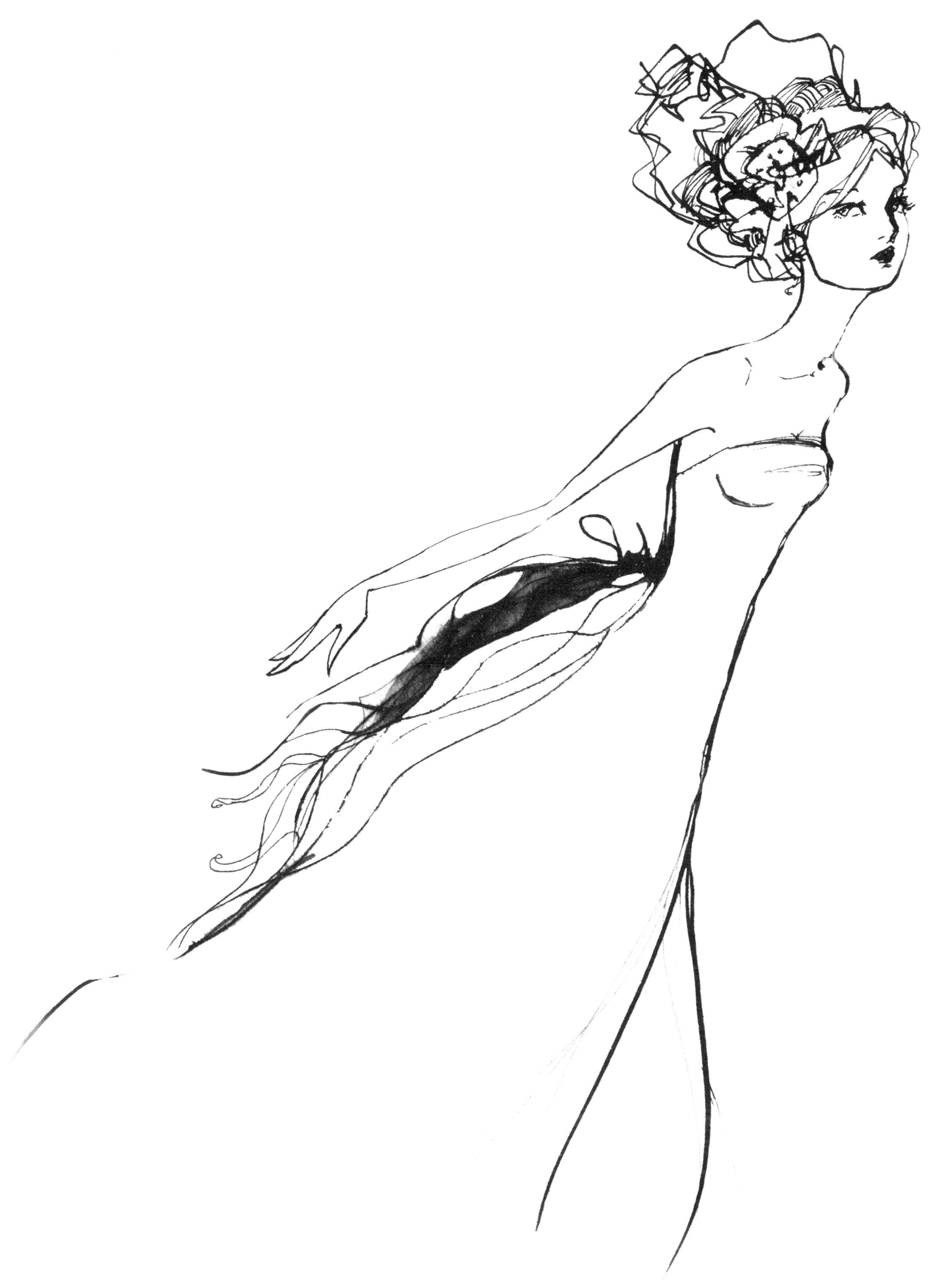

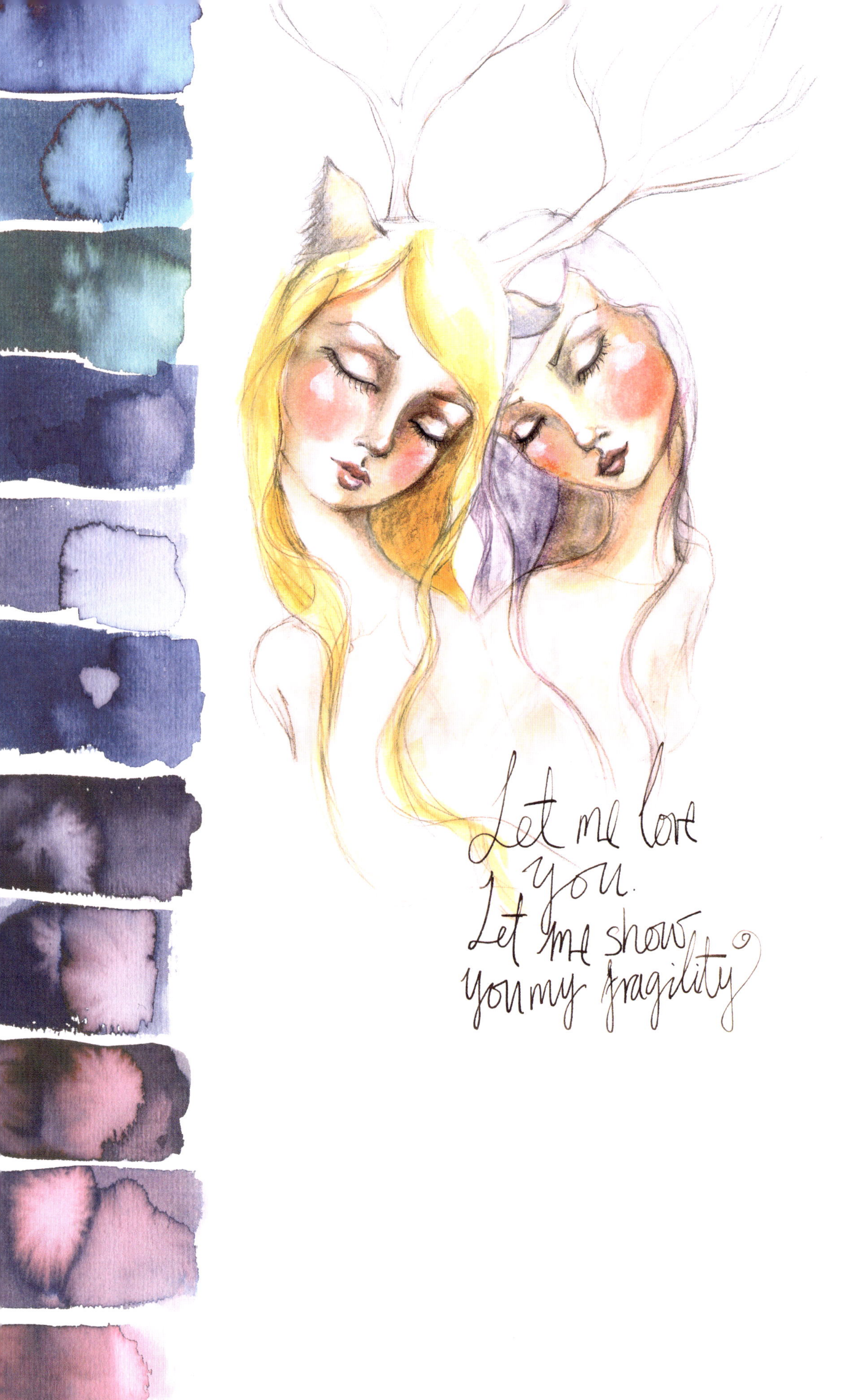
Let me love
you.
Let me show
you my fragility

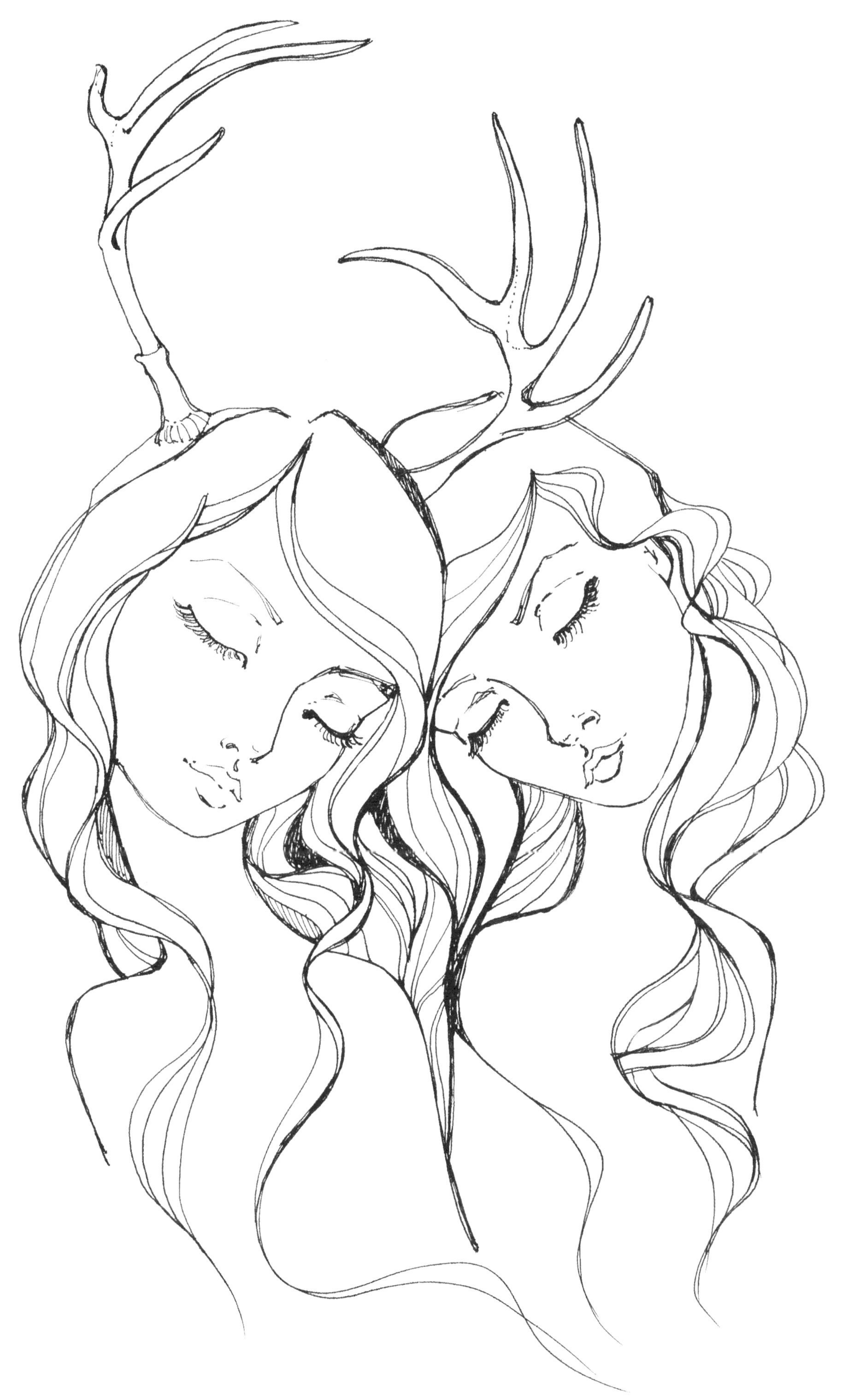

the moment we
set off in search
of our 'style'
it sets off in

search of us.

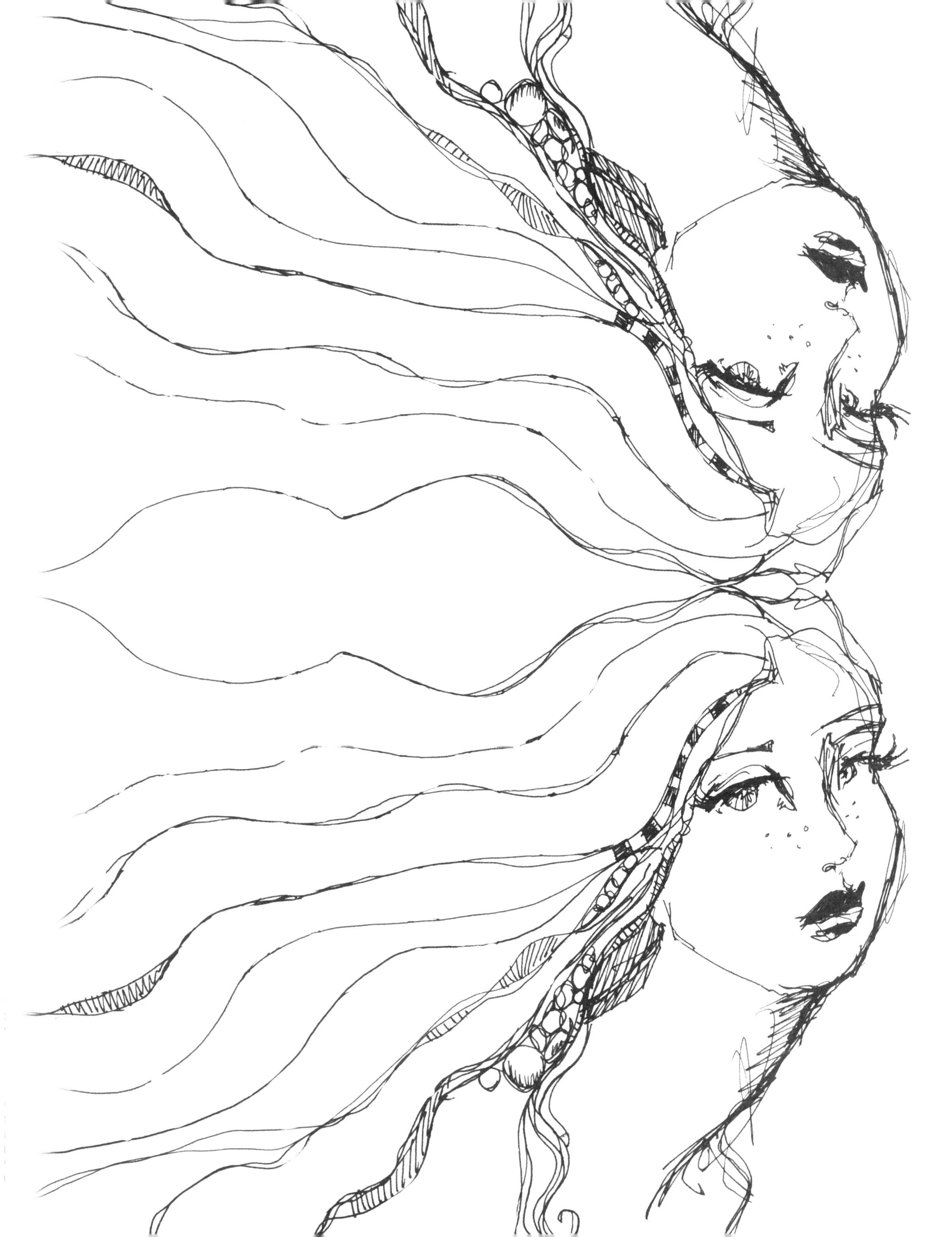

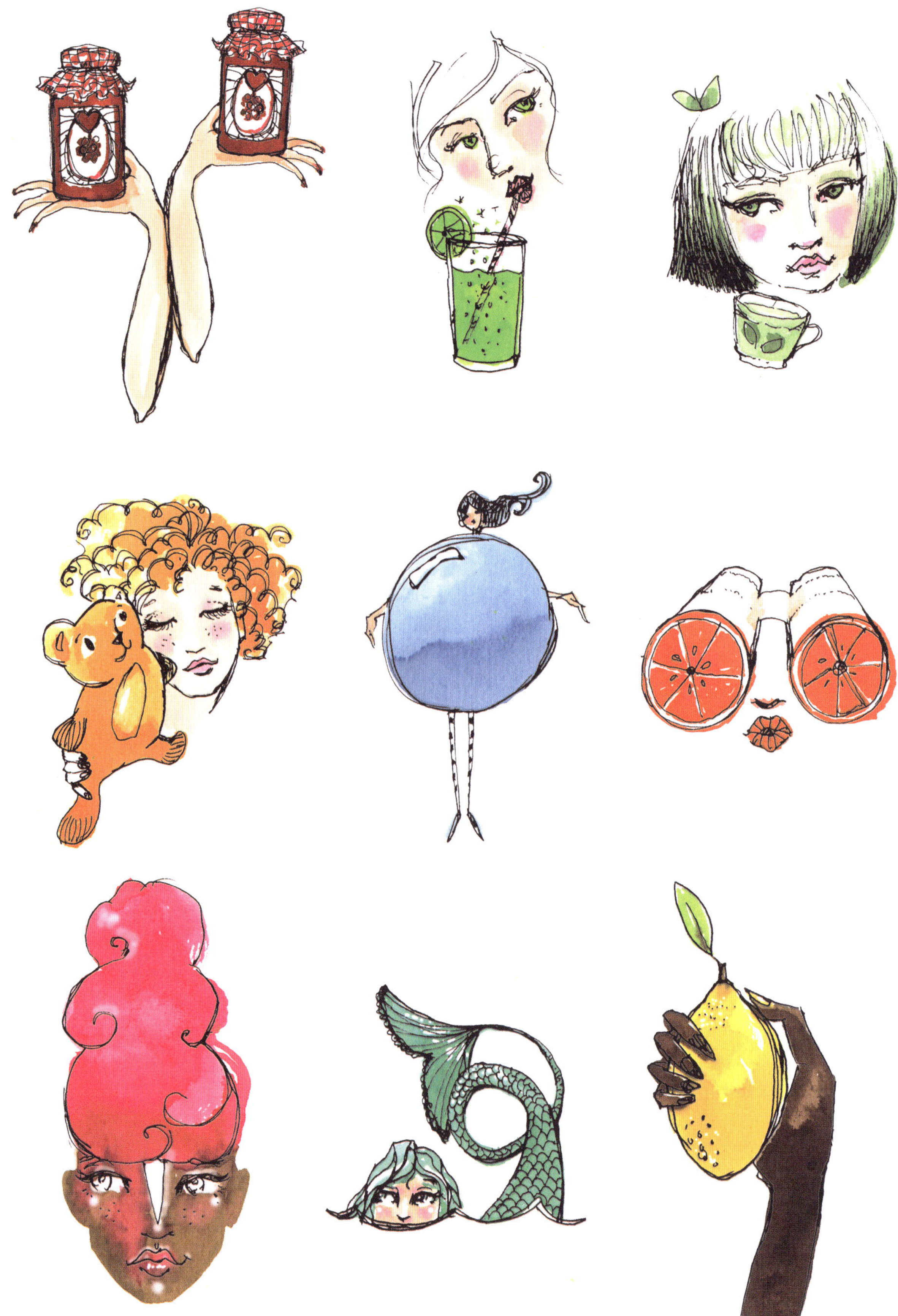

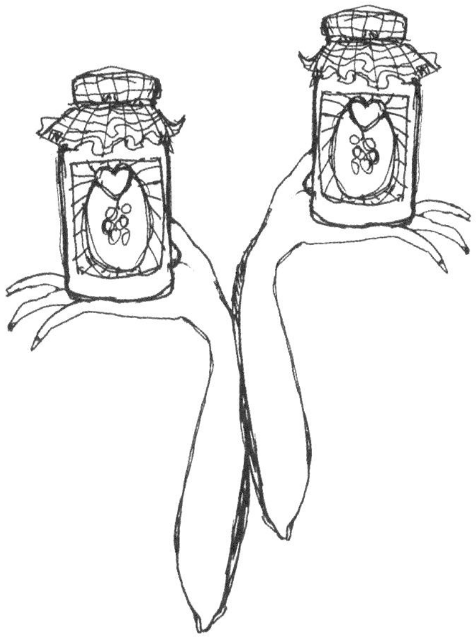

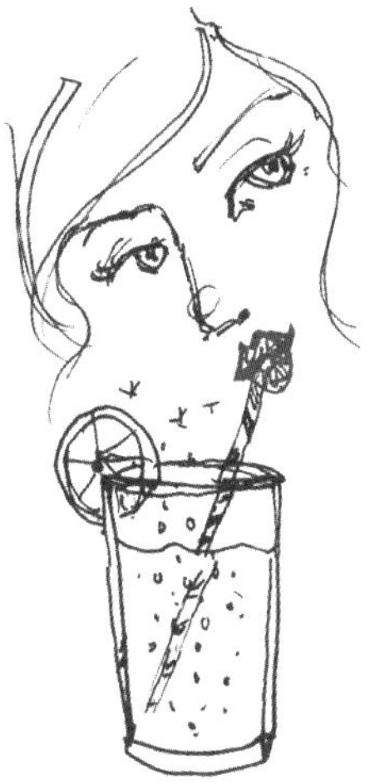

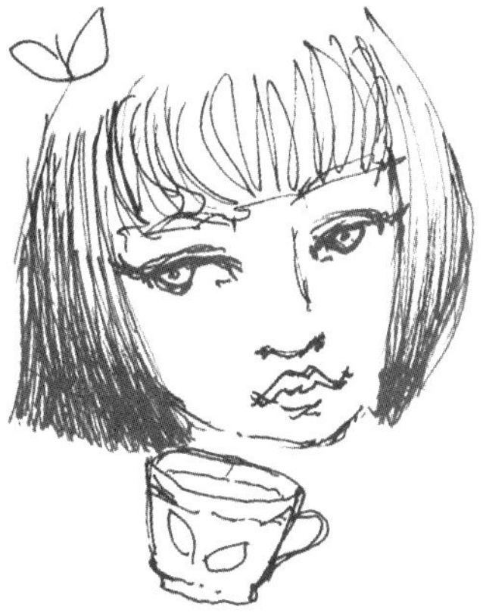

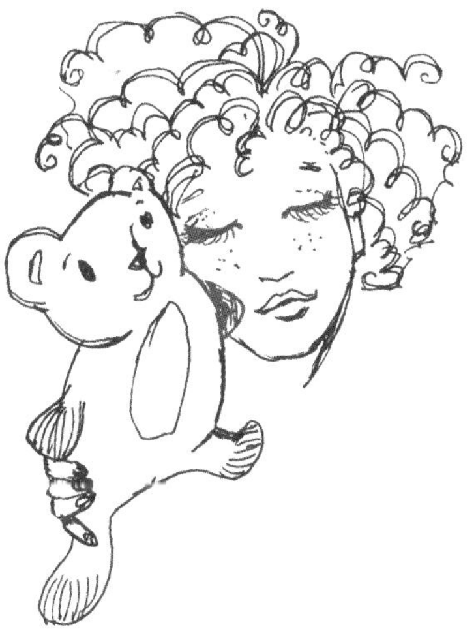

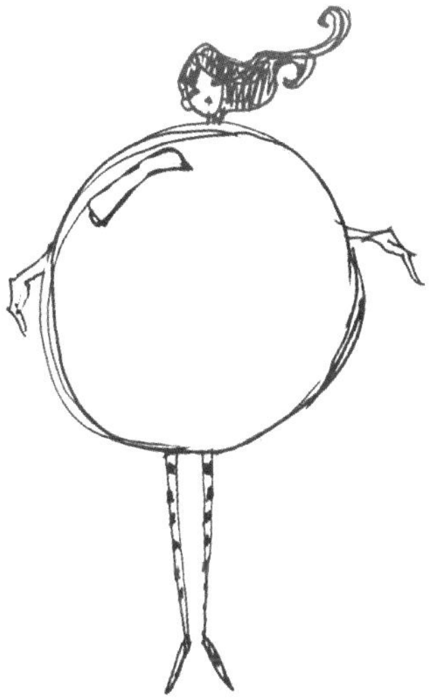

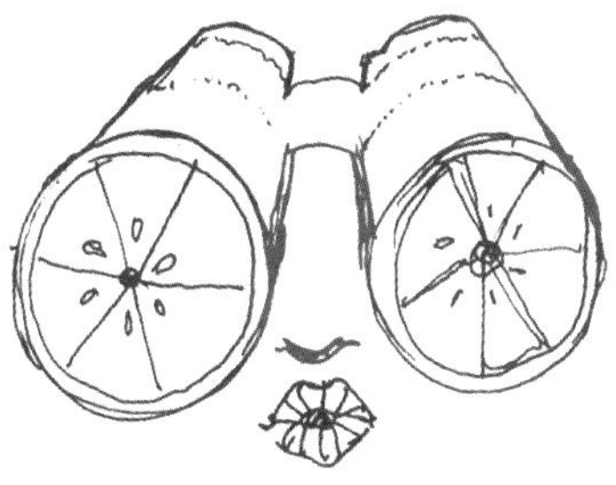

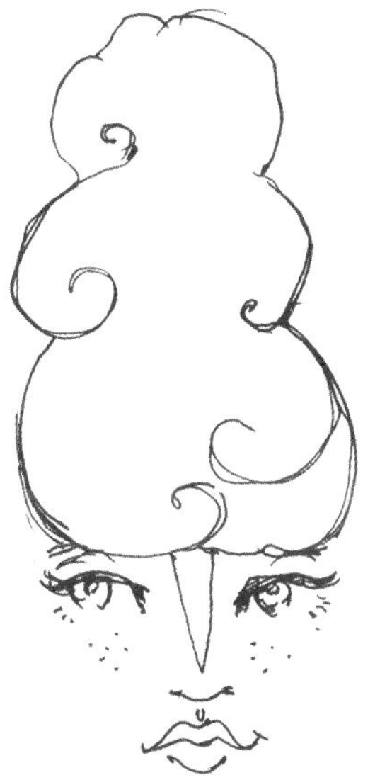

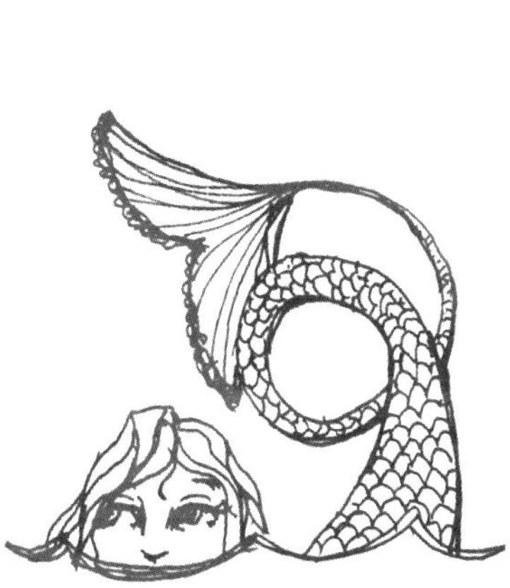

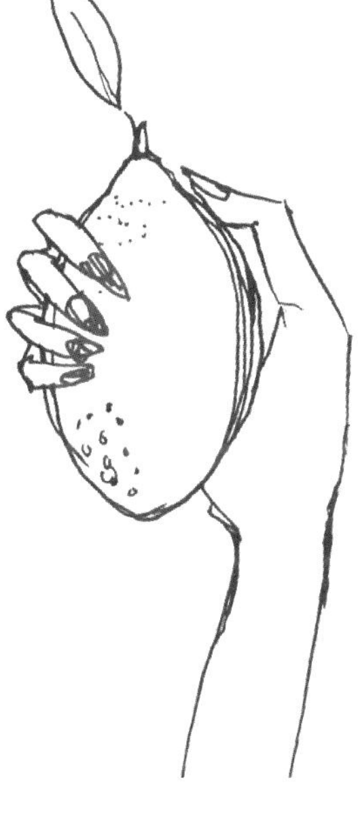

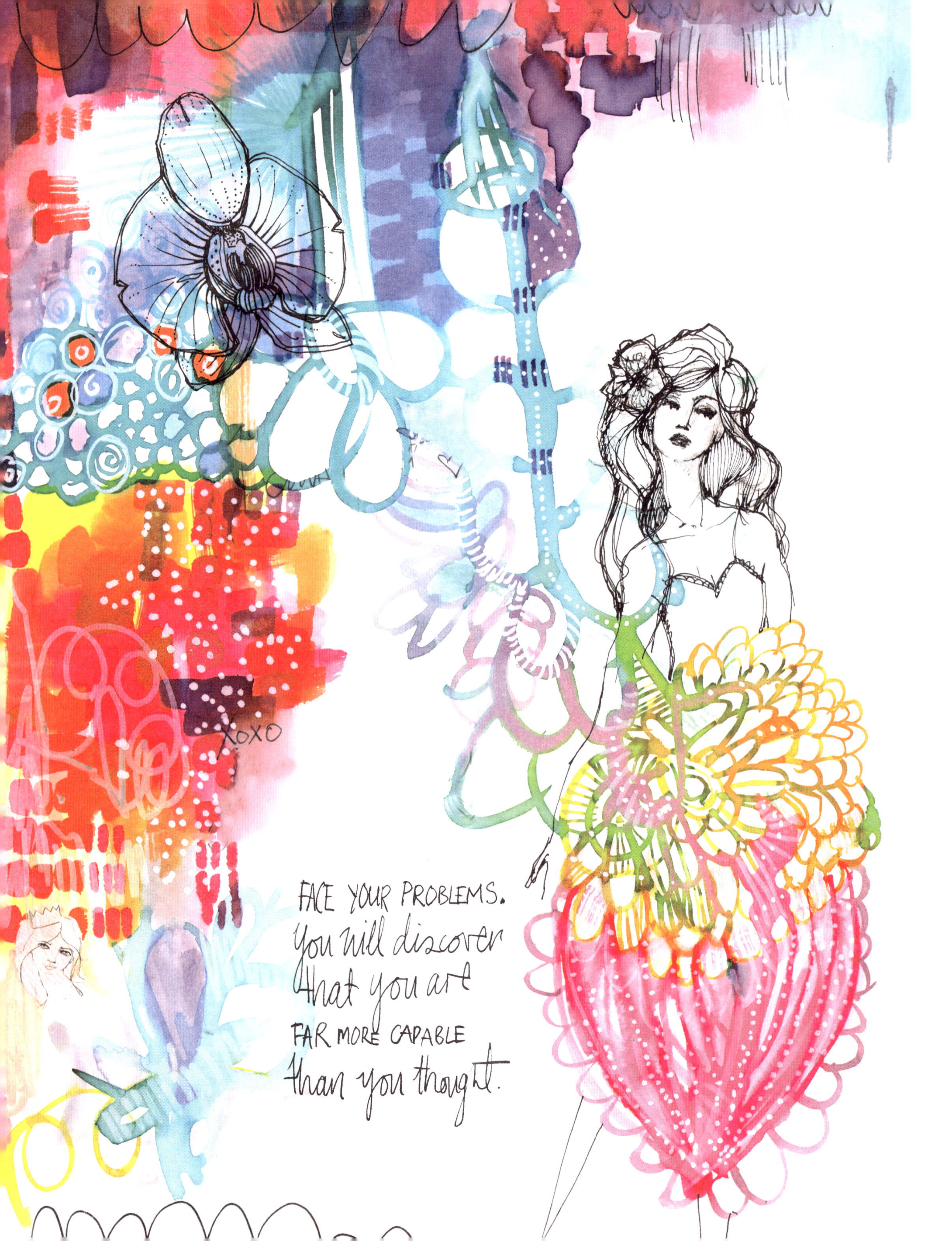

xoxo
FACE YOUR PROBLEMS.
You will discover
that you are
FAR MORE CAPABLE
than you thought.

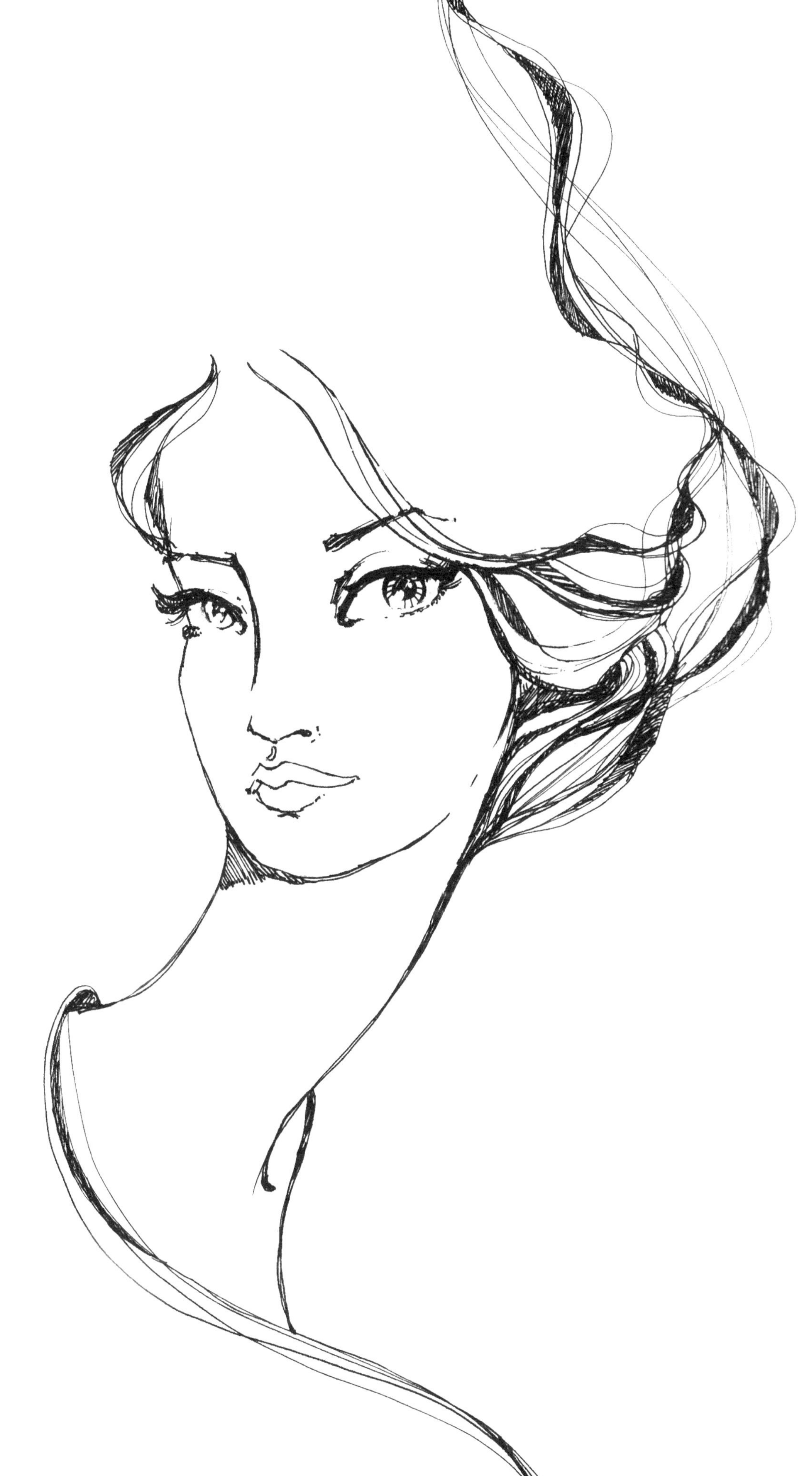

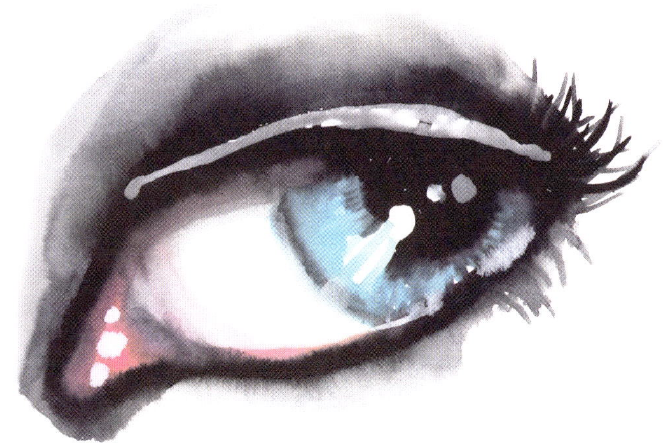
The Artist has the Universe in their MIND & HANDS

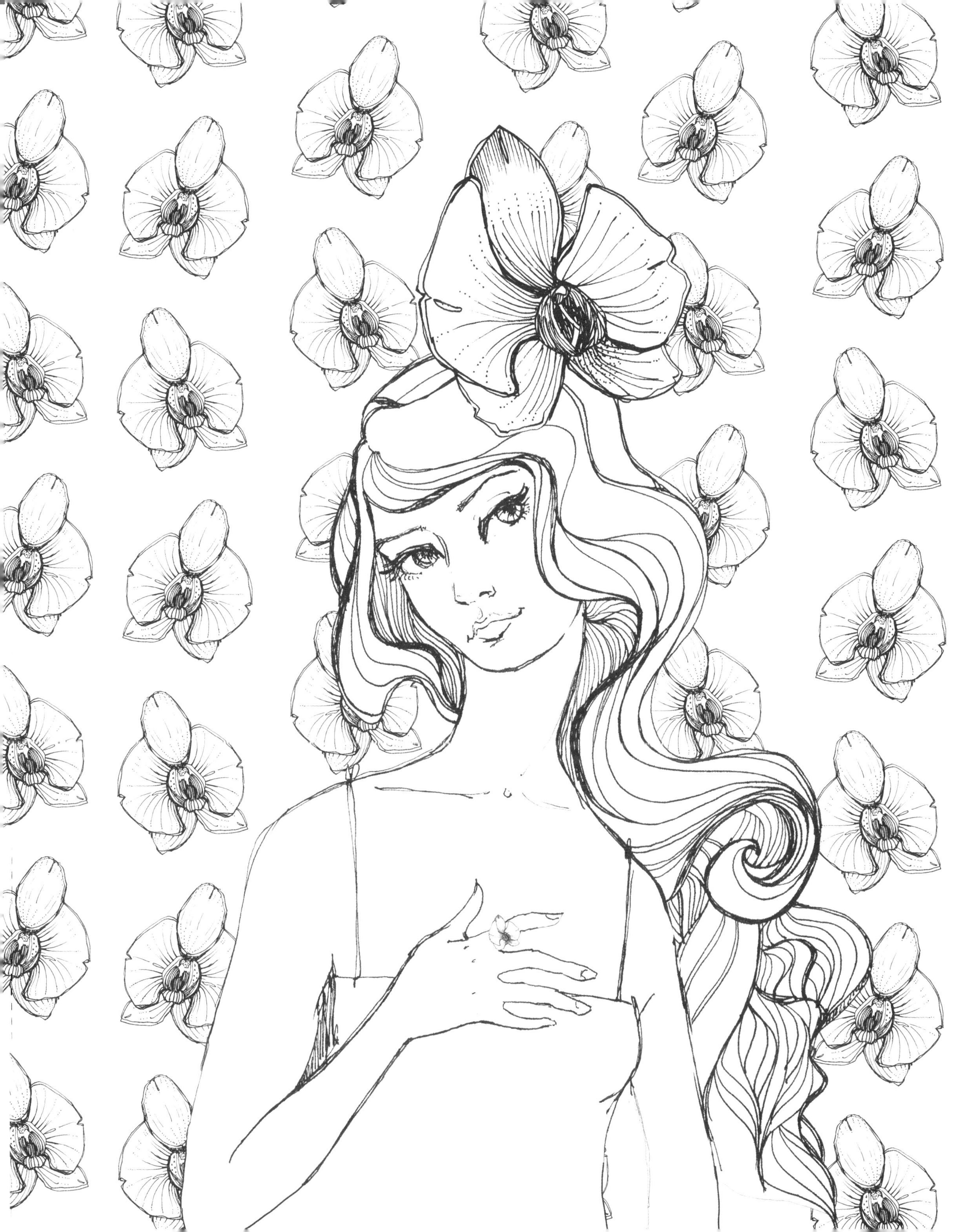

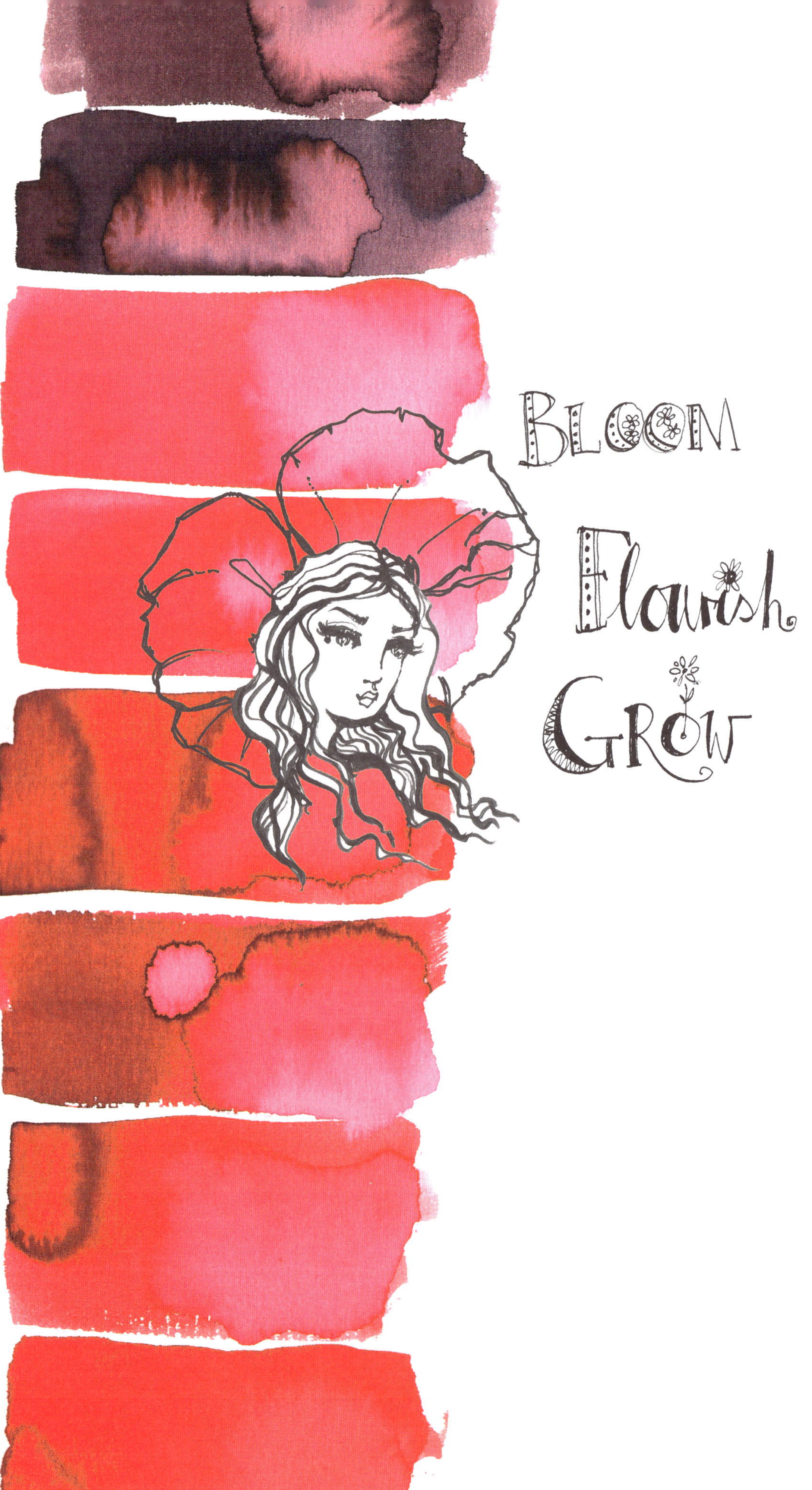

Bloom
Flourish
Grow

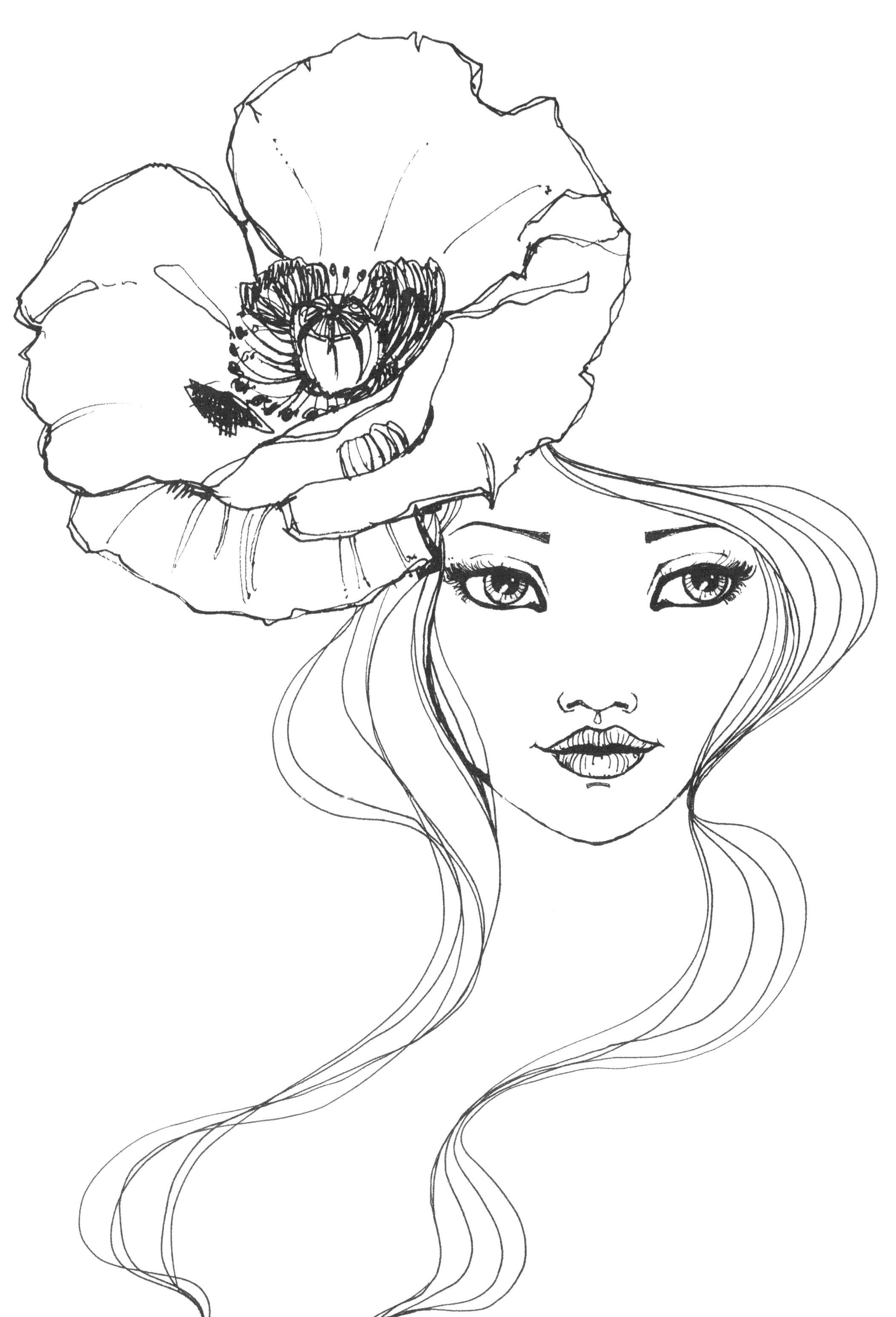

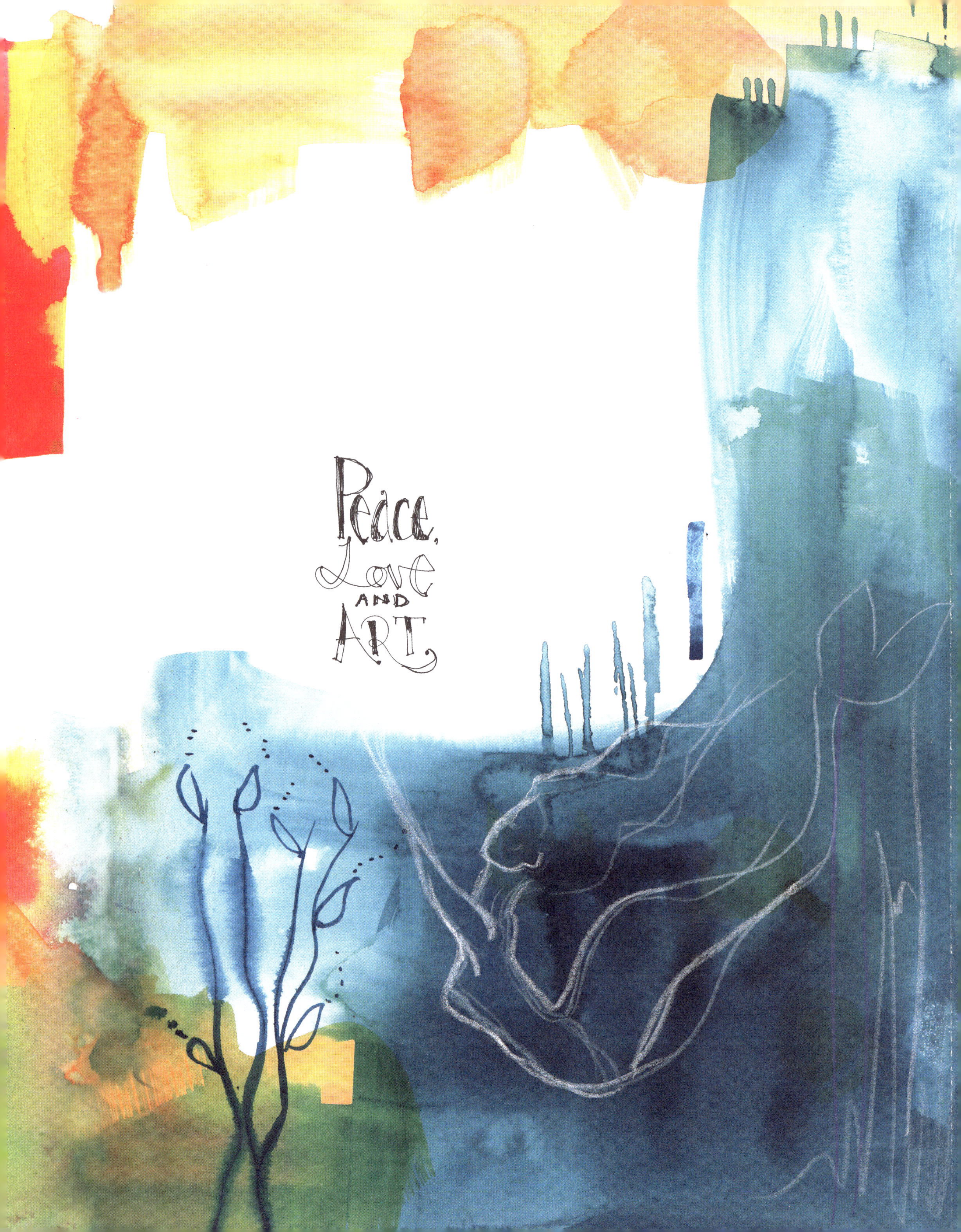
Peace,
Love
AND
ART

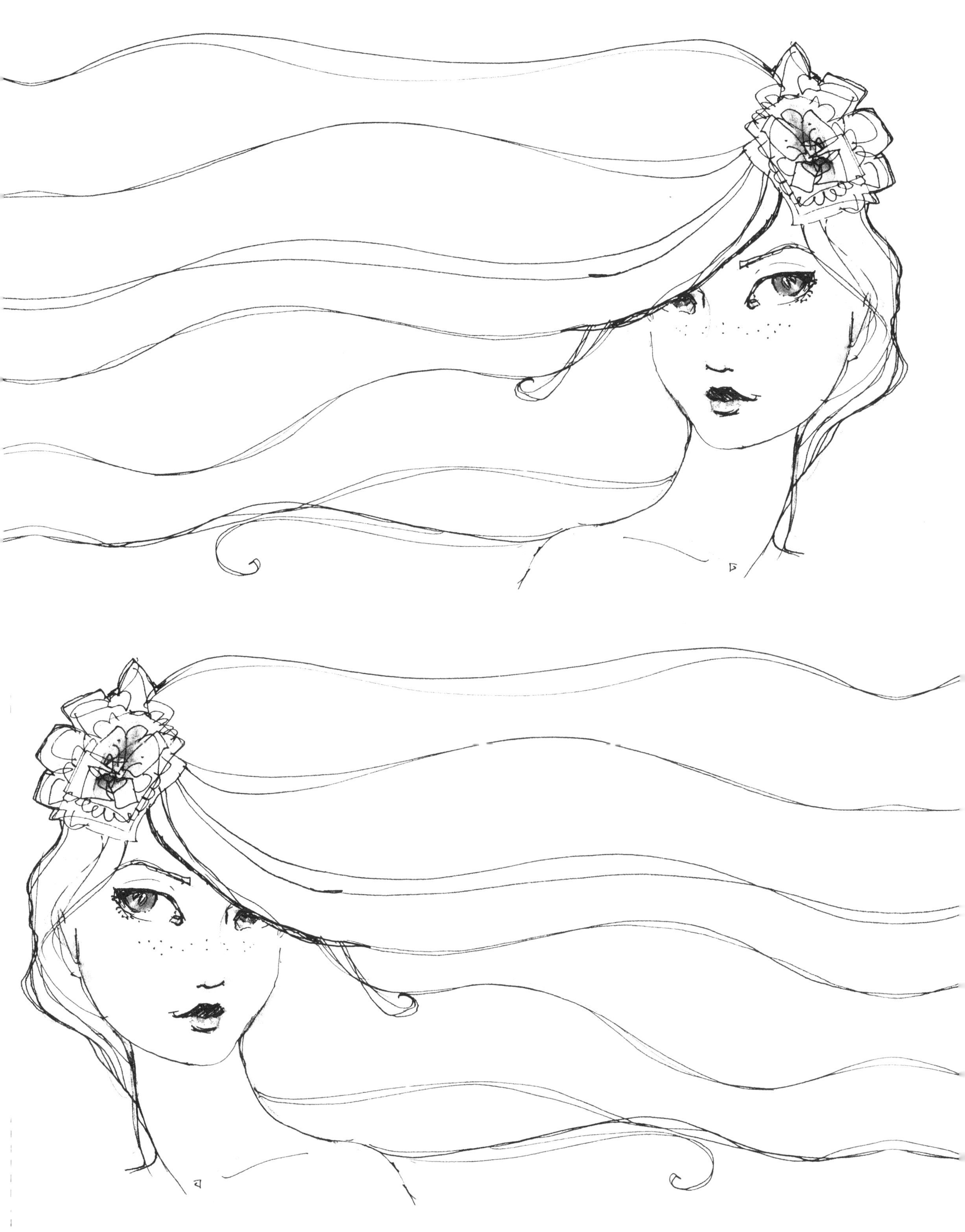

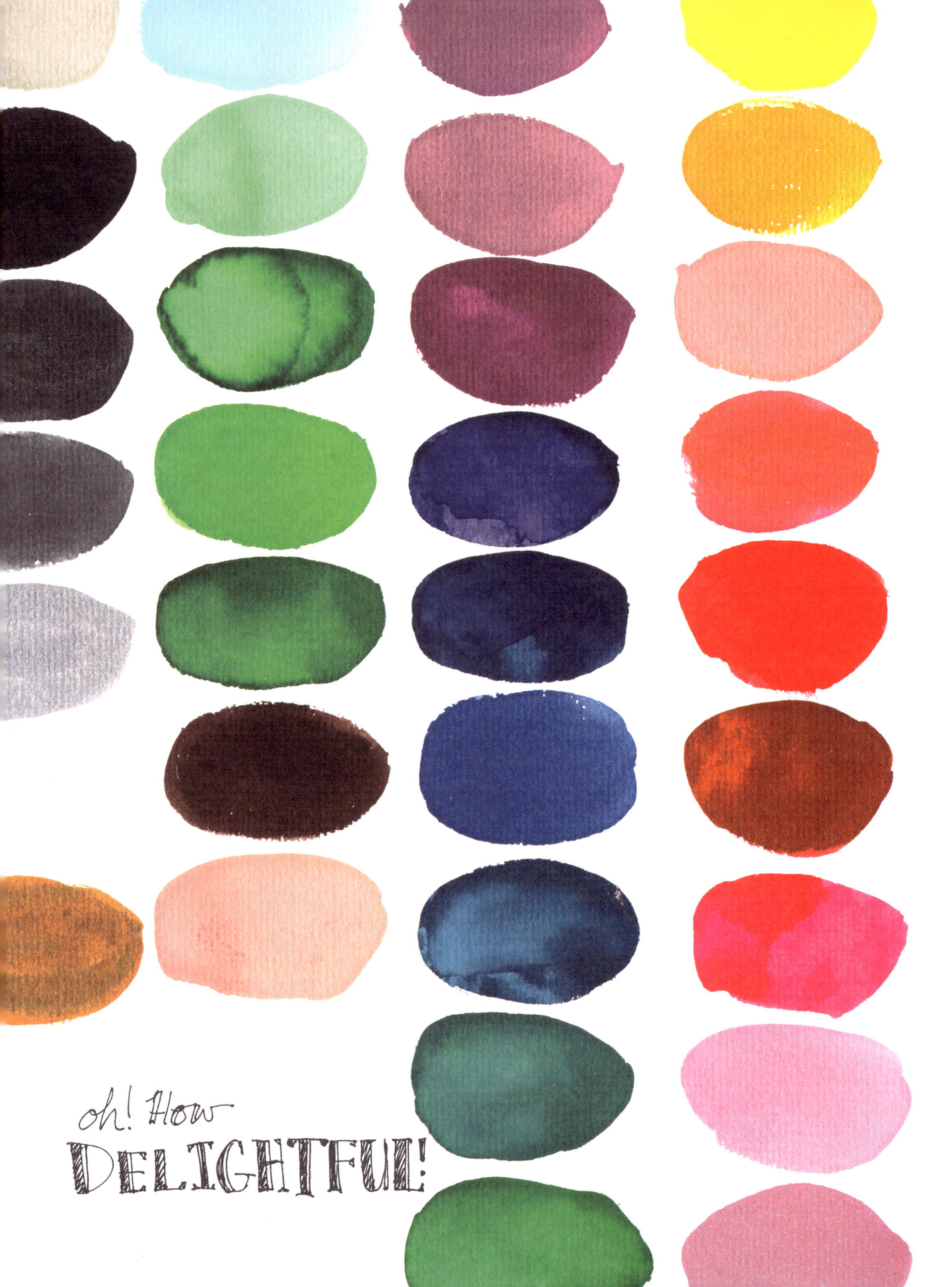

oh! How
DELIGHTFUL!

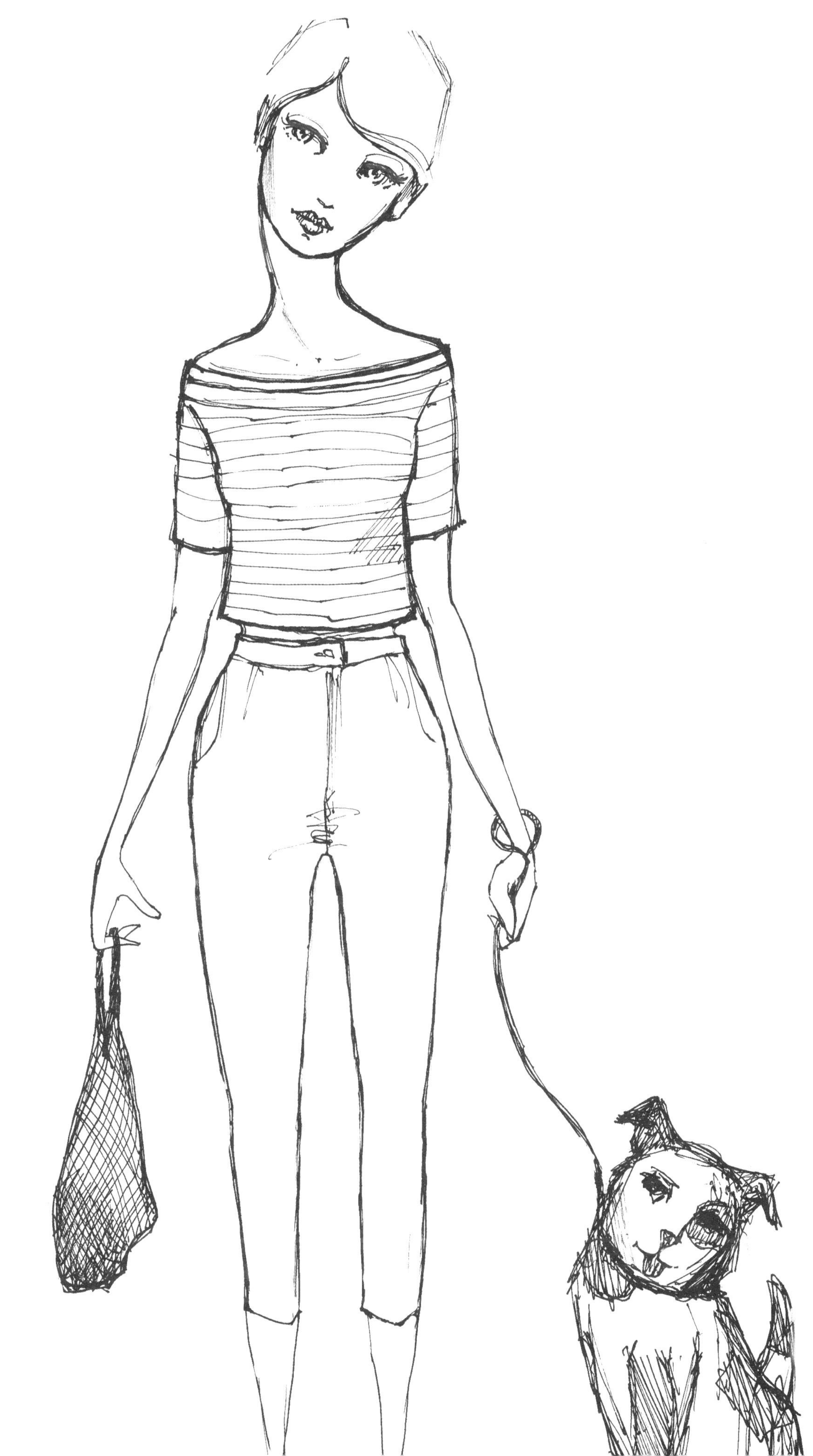

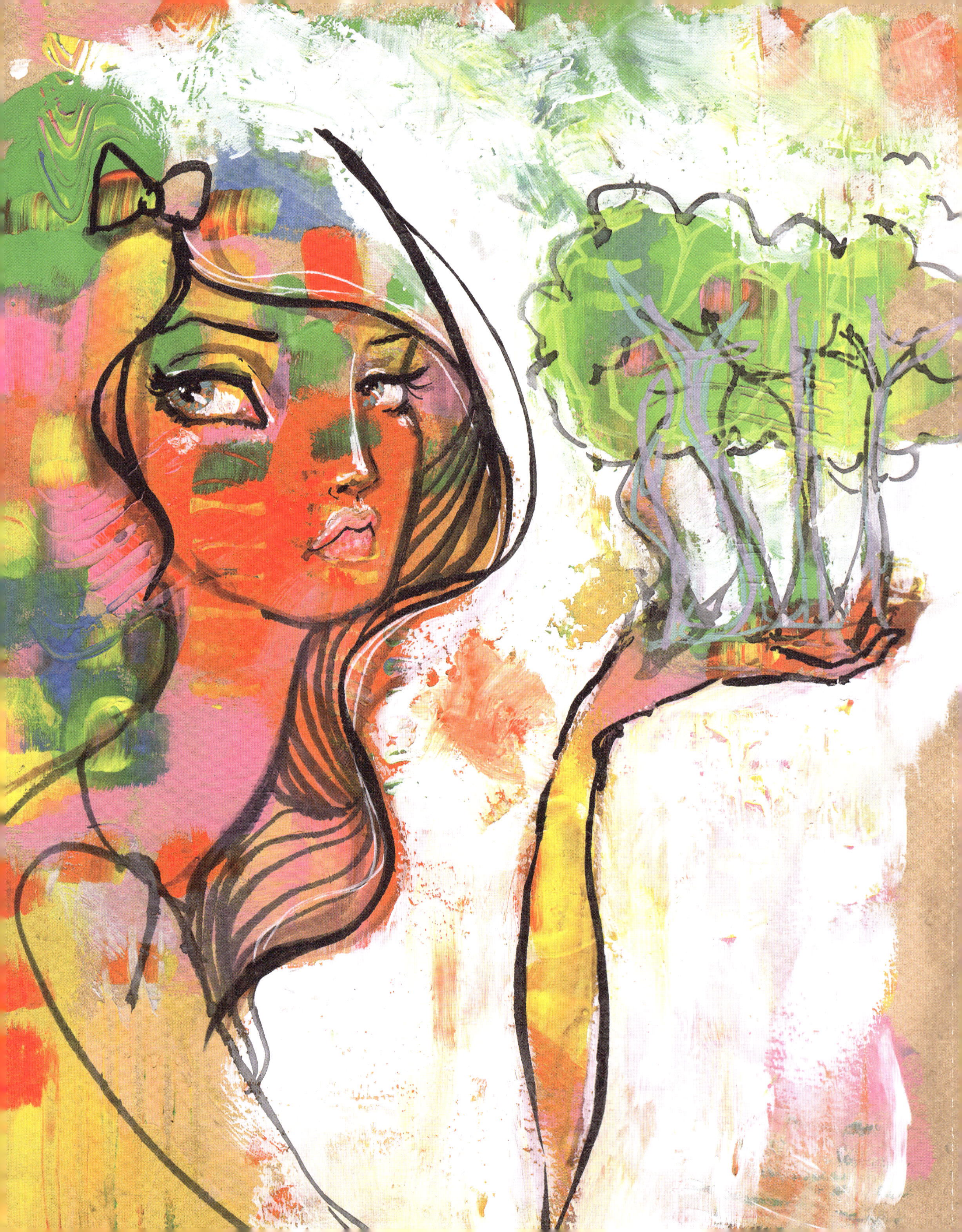

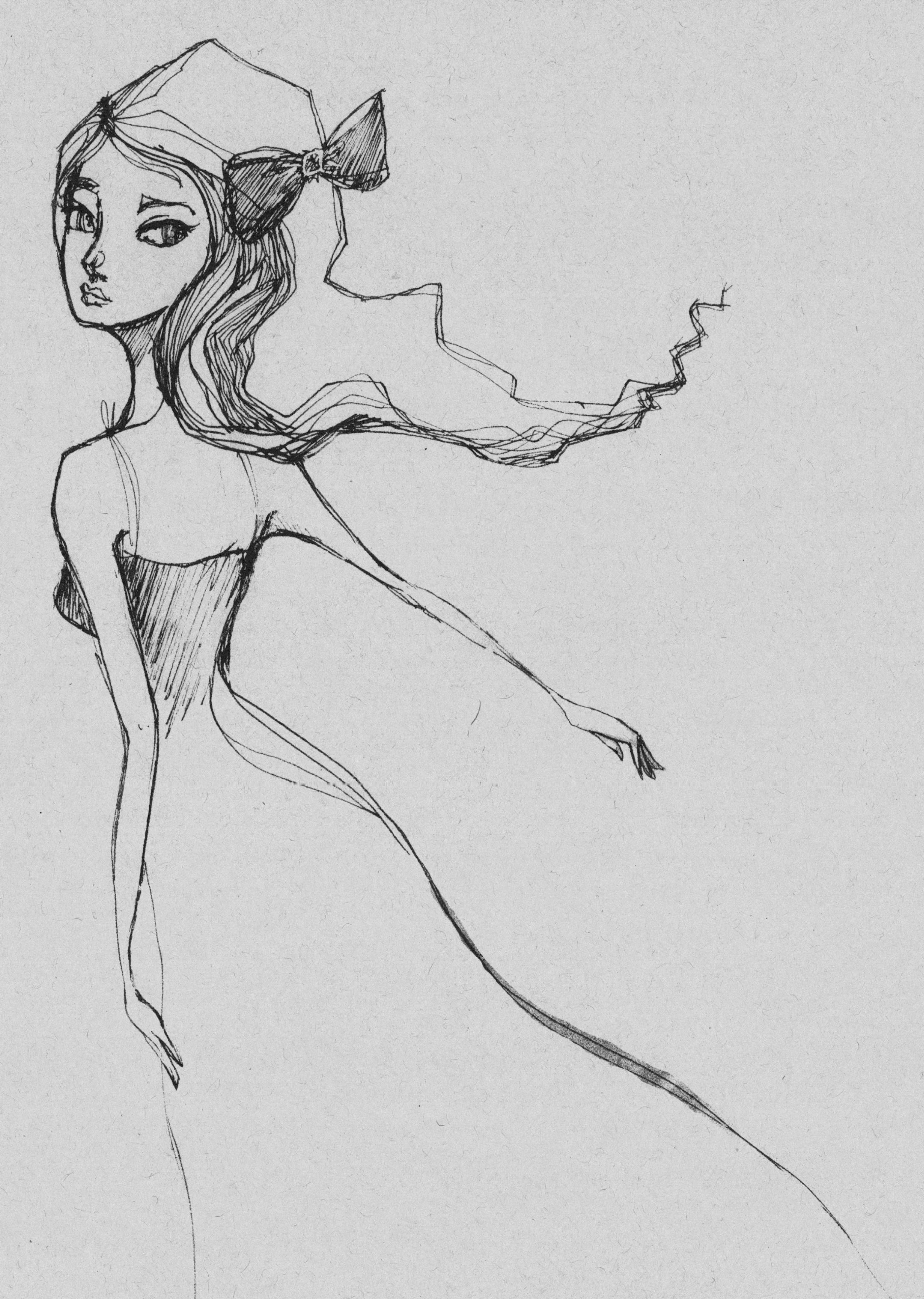

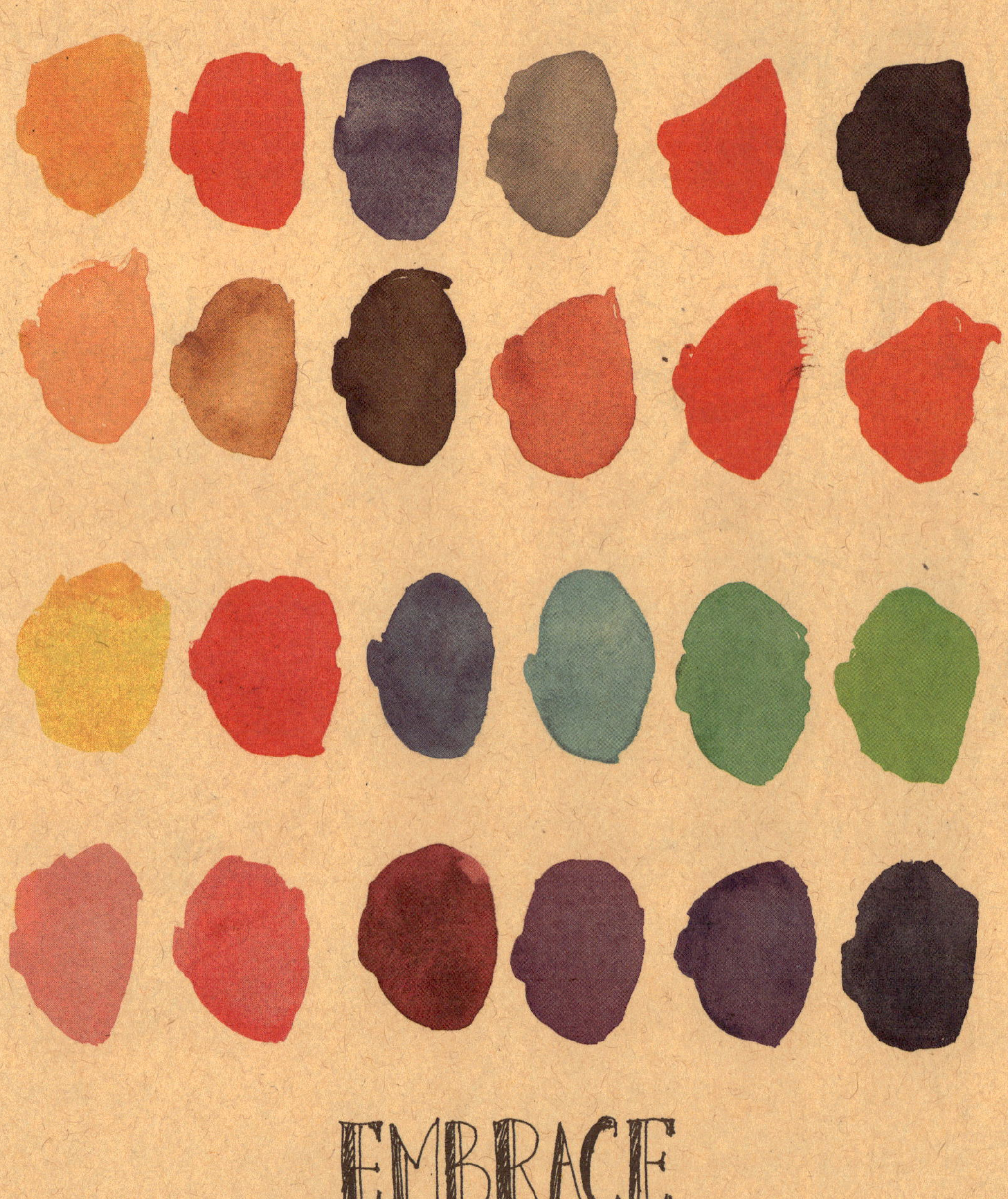

EMBRACE
the PROCESS

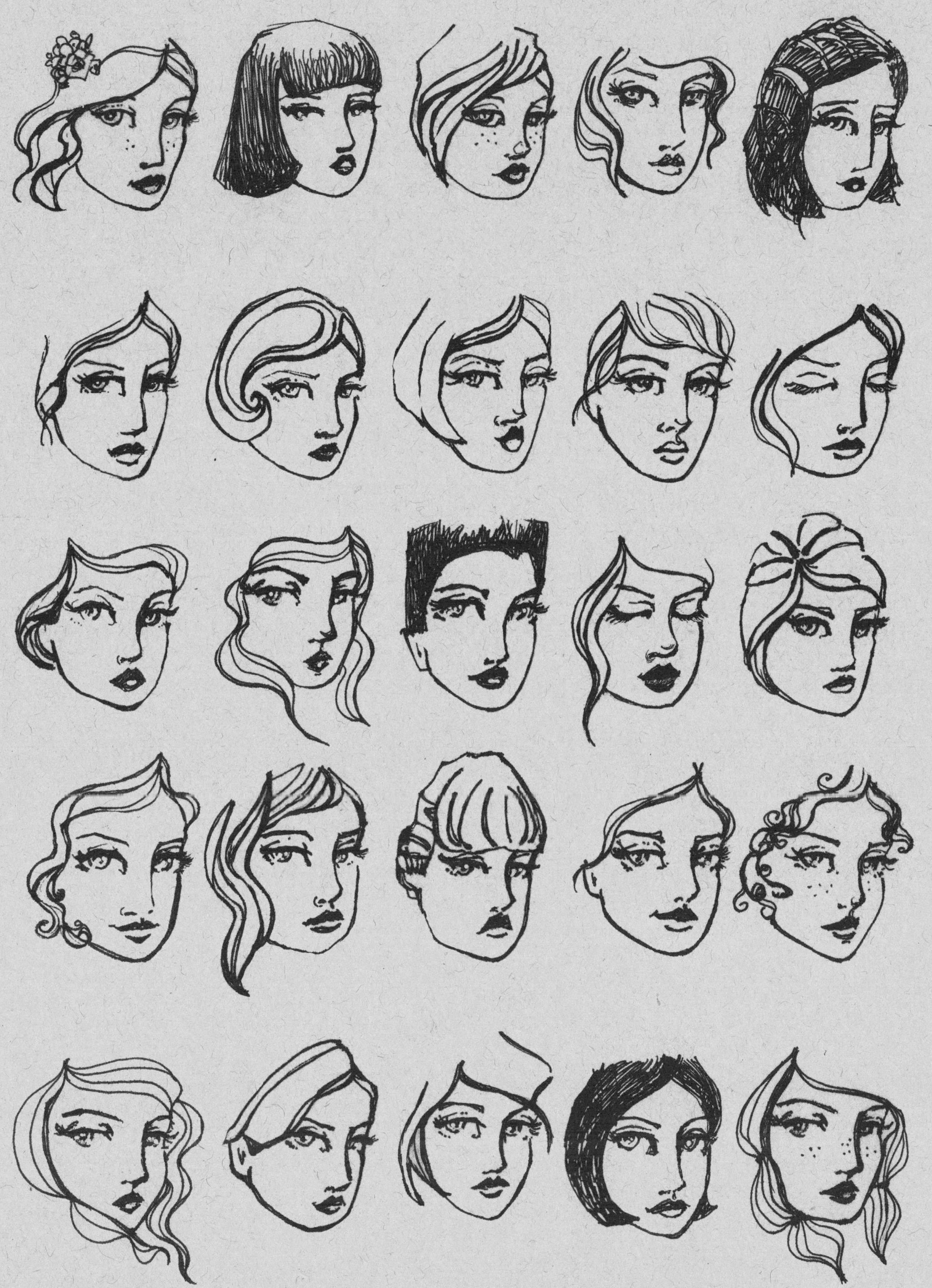

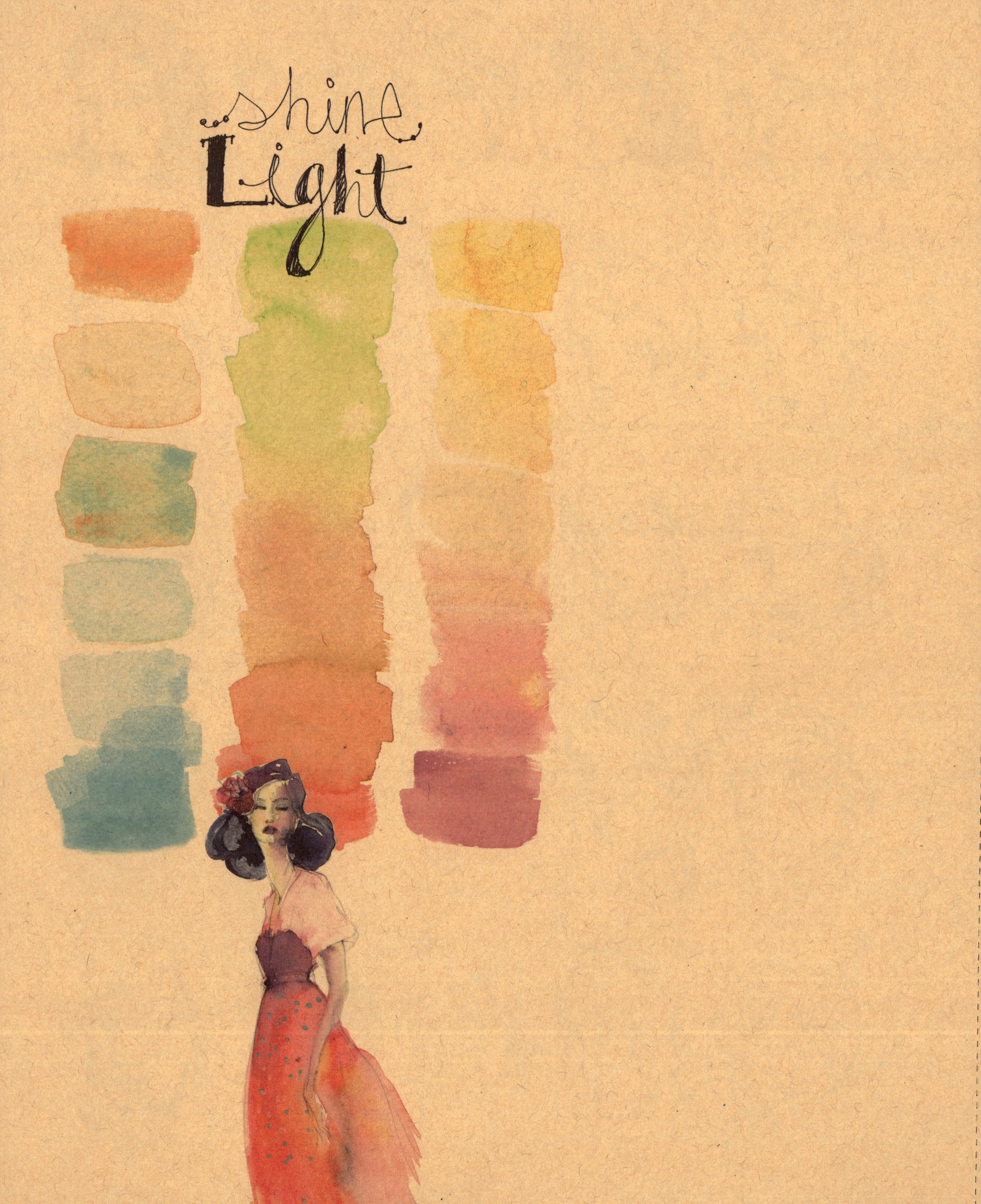

shine
Light

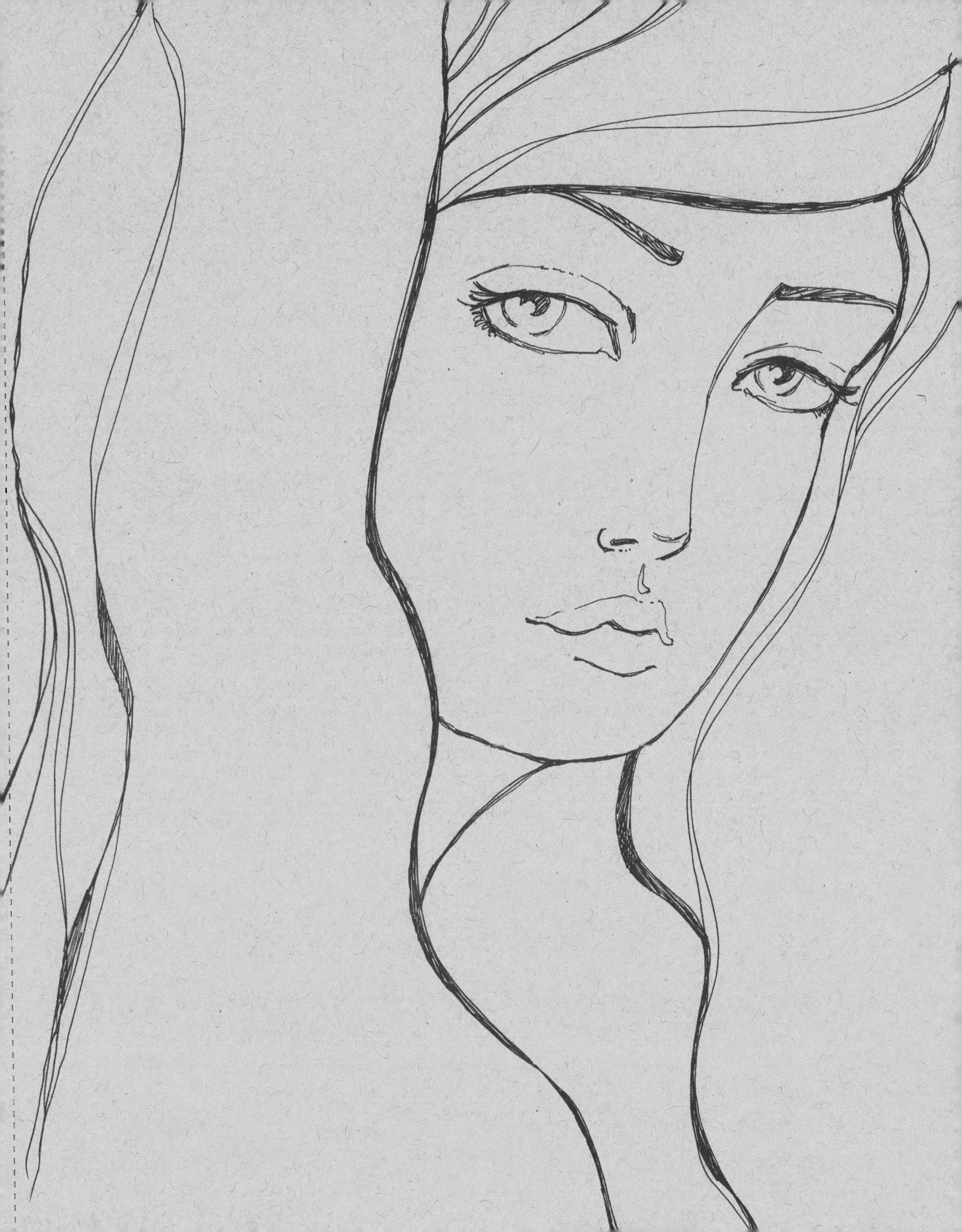

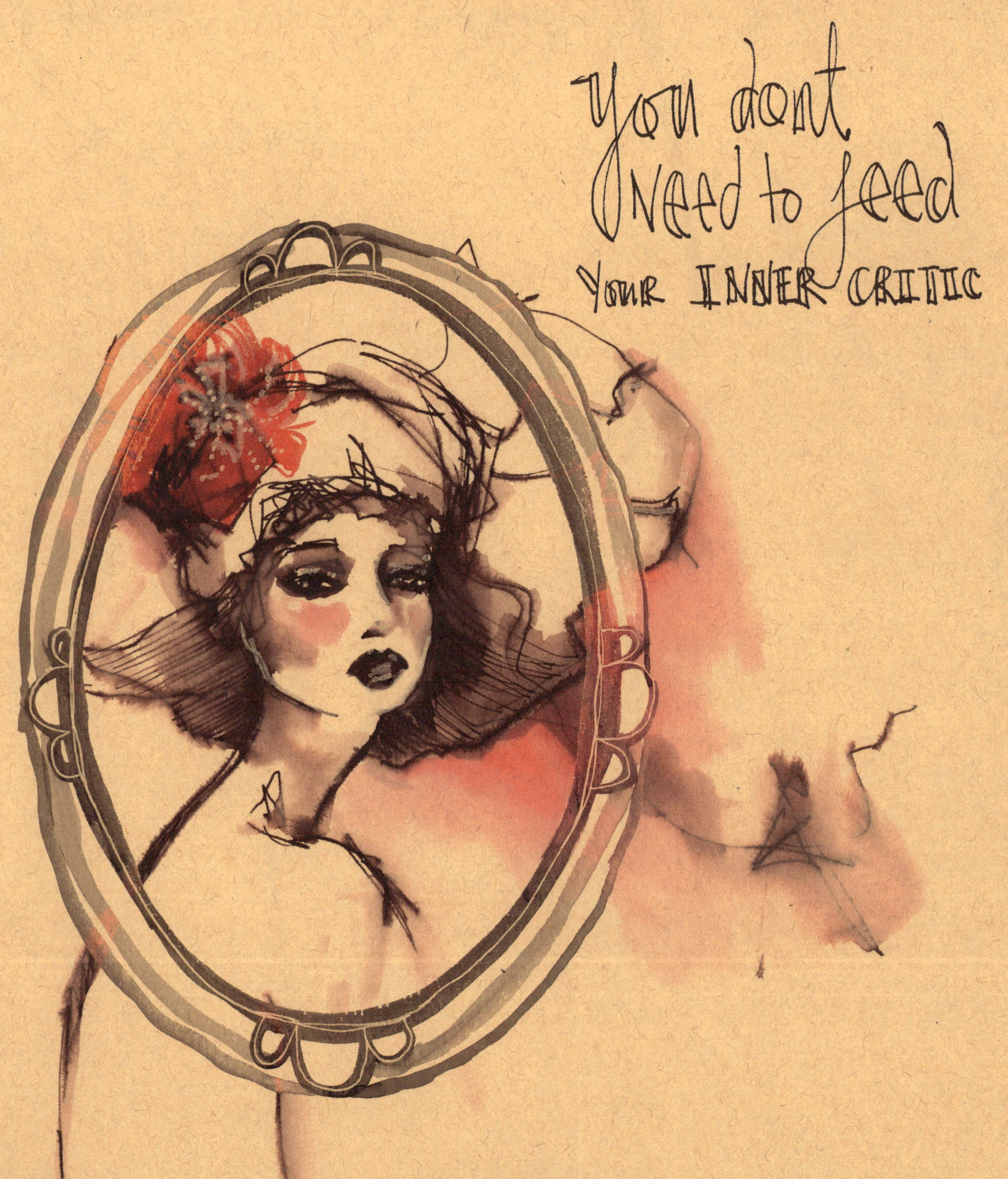
You dont
need to feed
your INNER CRITIC

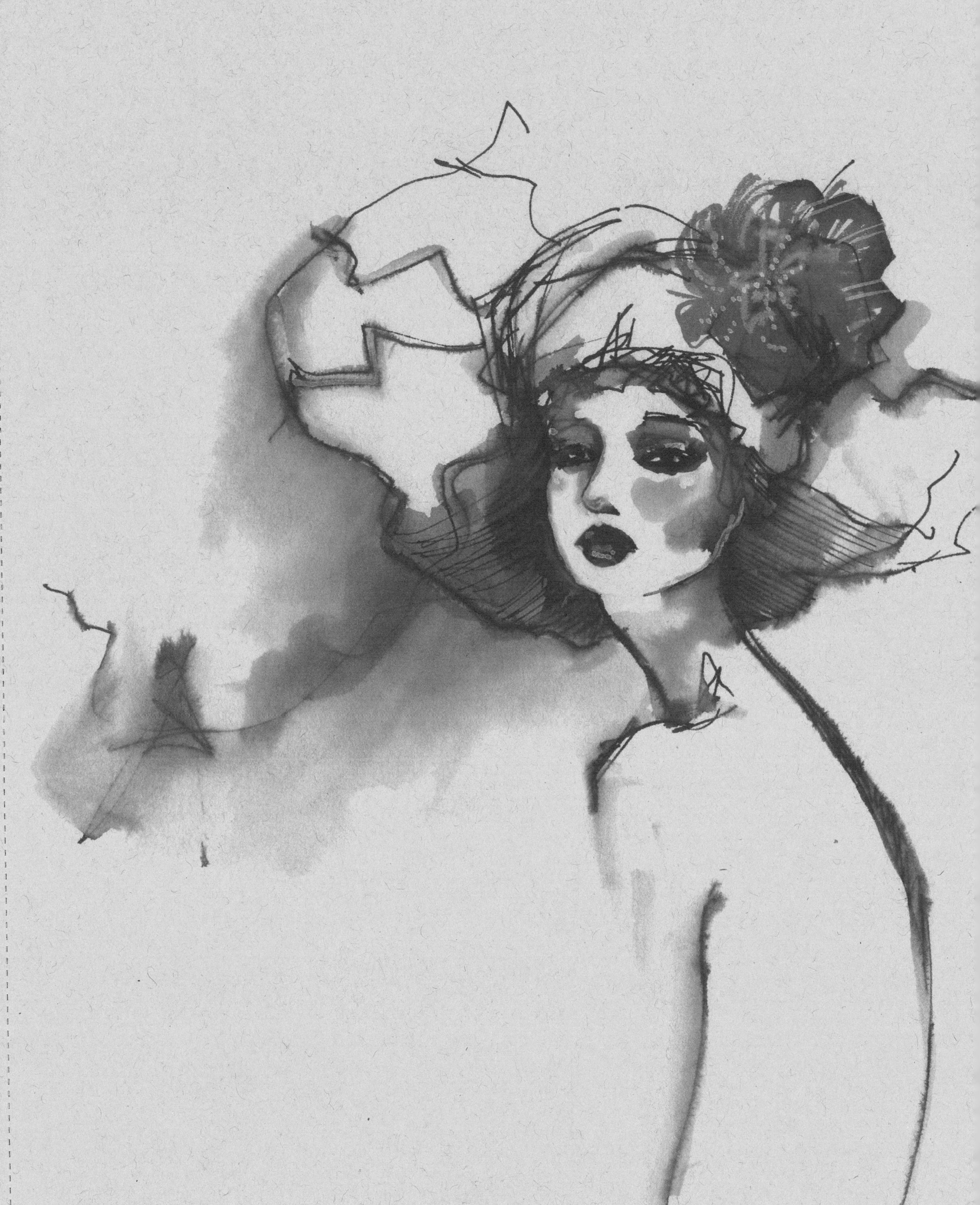

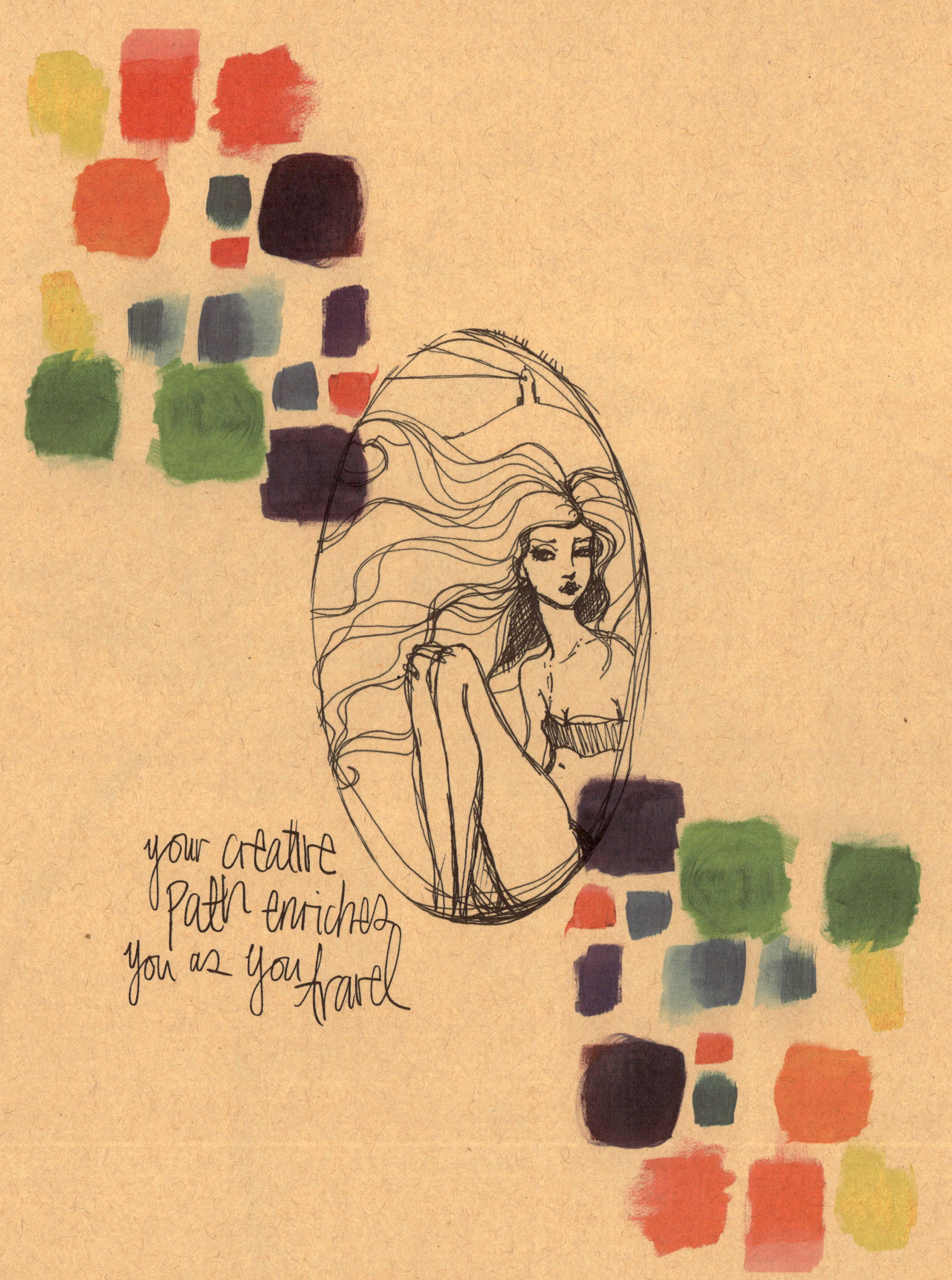

your creative
path enriches
you as you travel

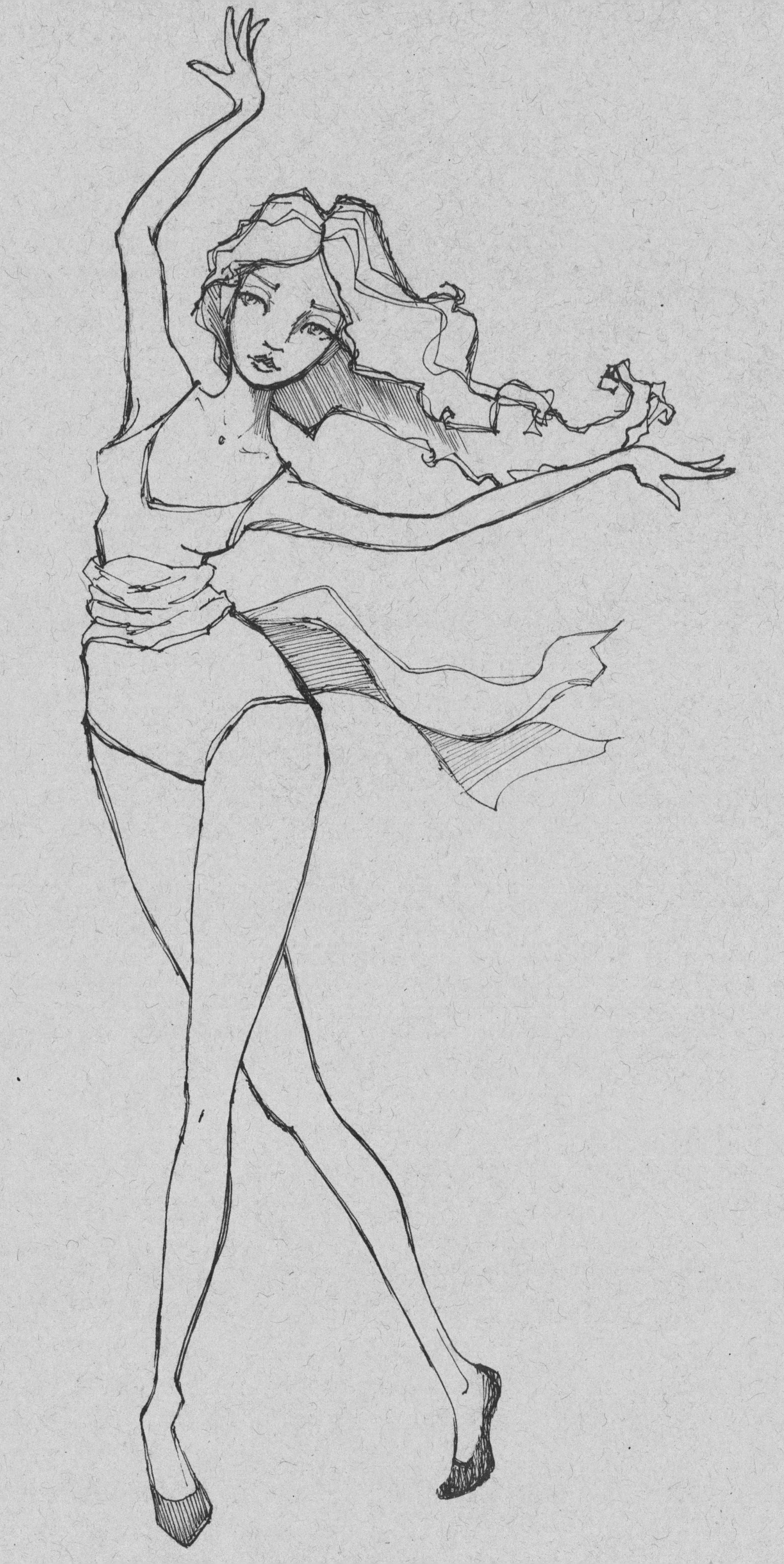

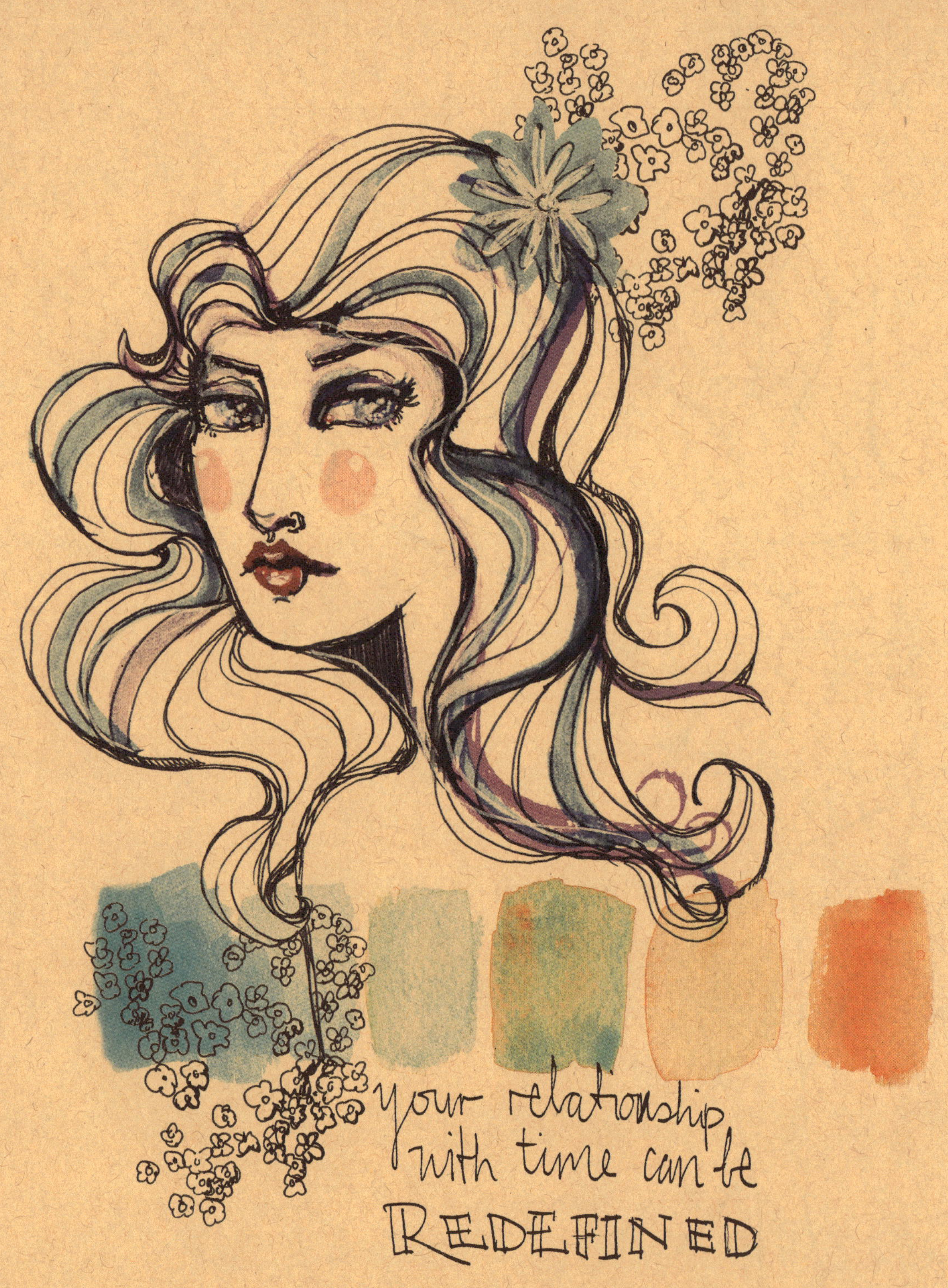
your relationship
with time can be
REDEFINED

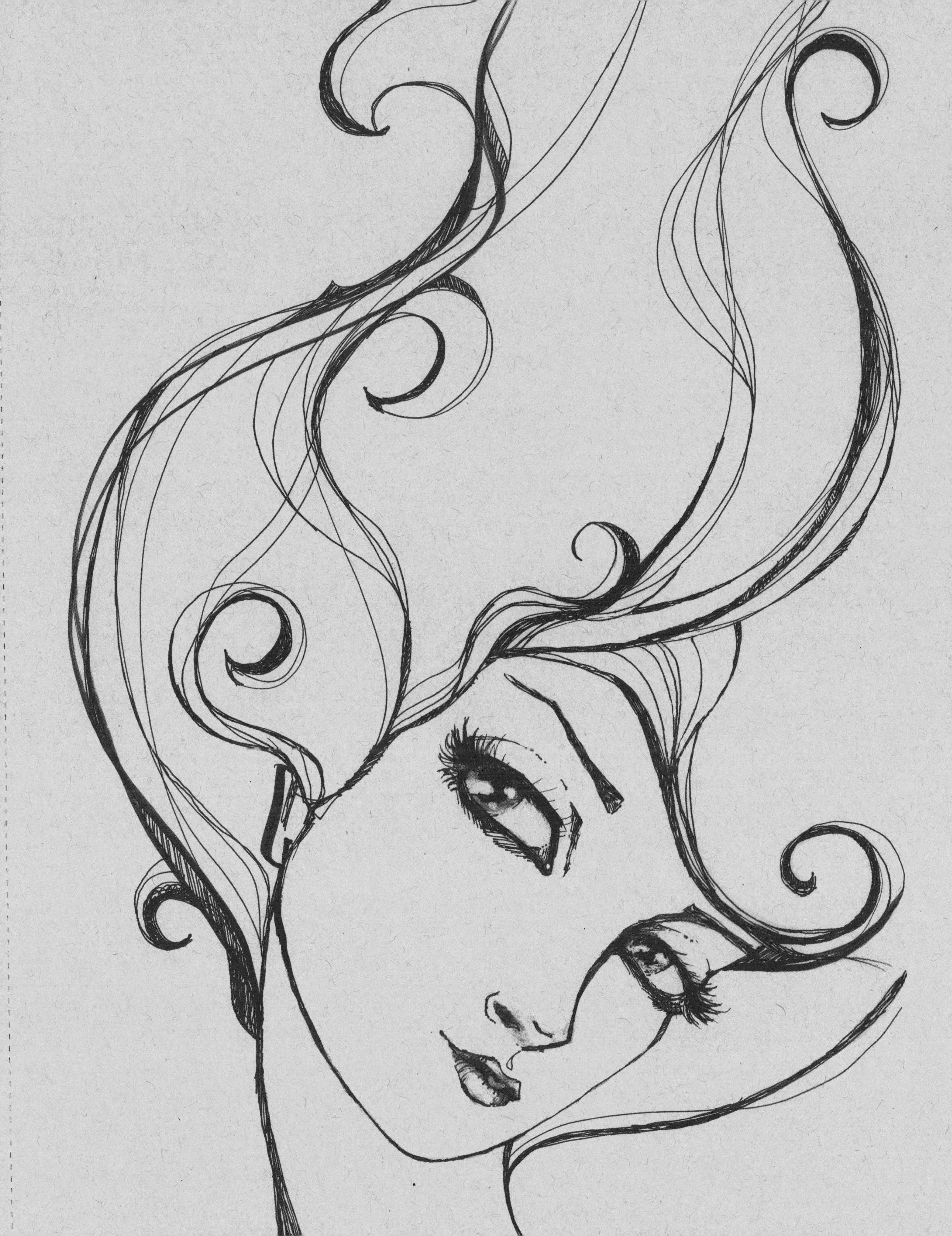

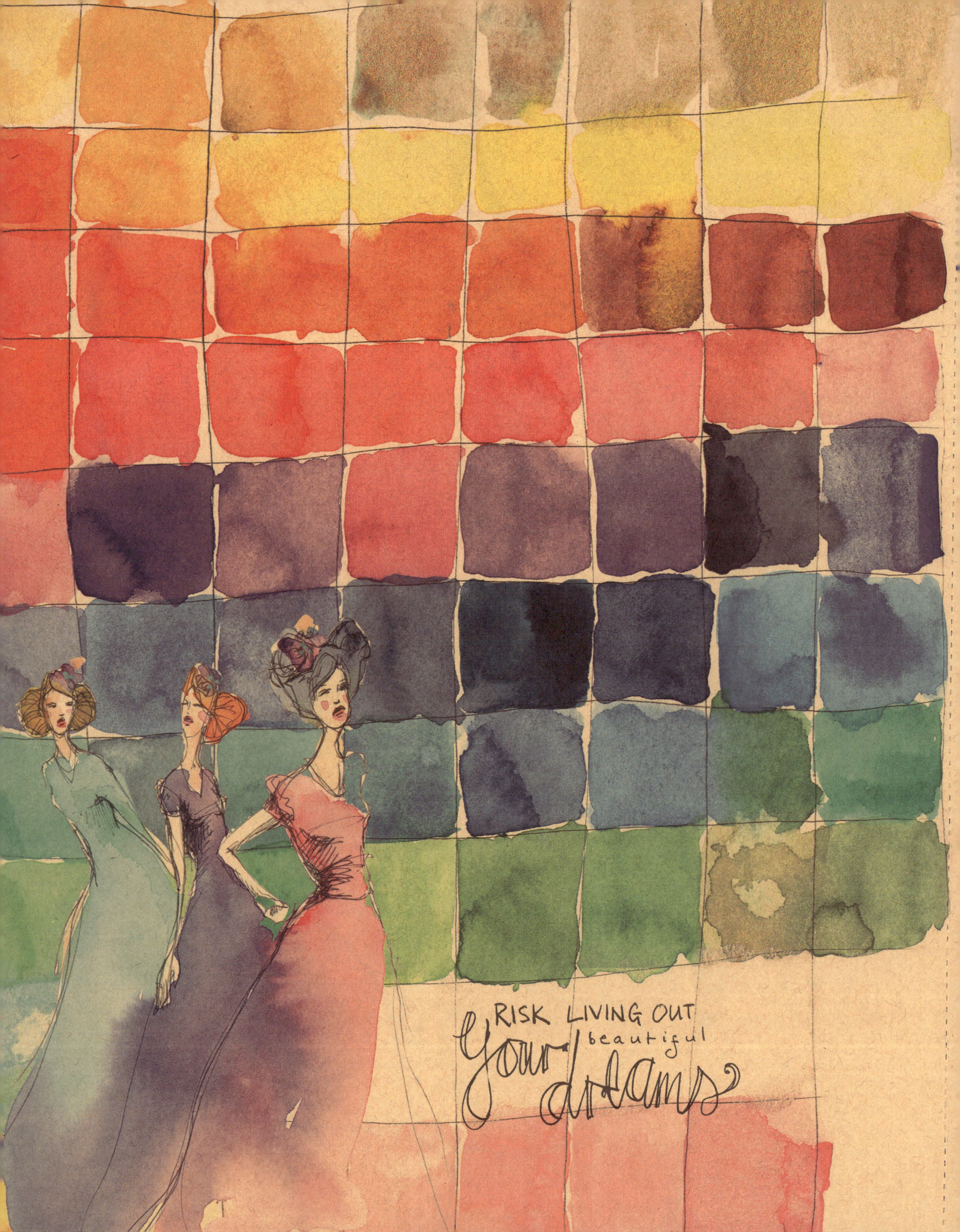

RISK LIVING OUT
your beautiful dreams

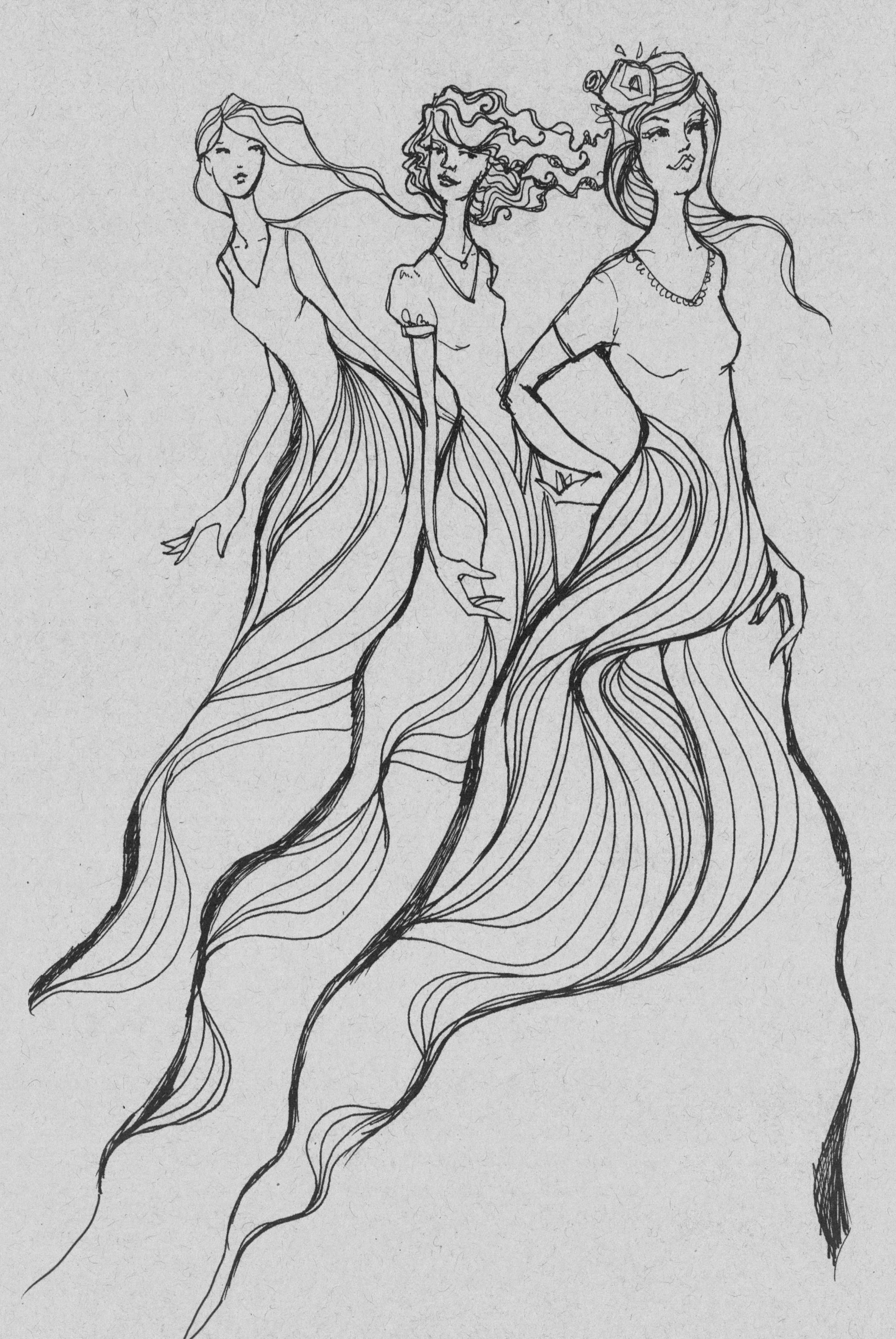

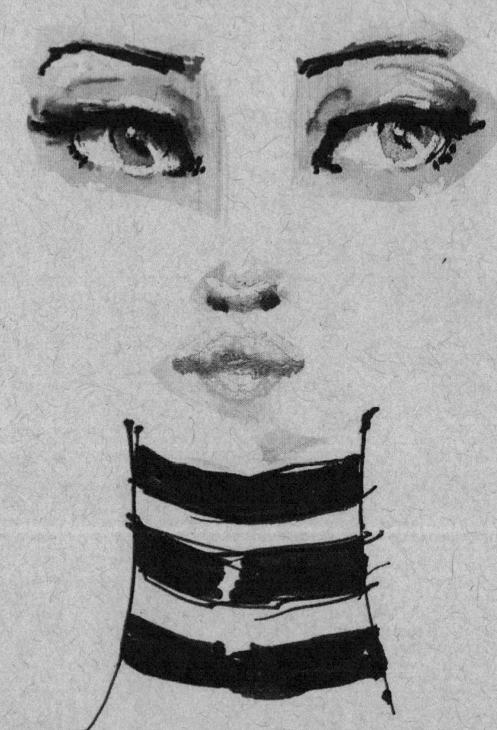

Know what you want.
Keep your eyes open.
Noone can hit their target
with closed eyes.

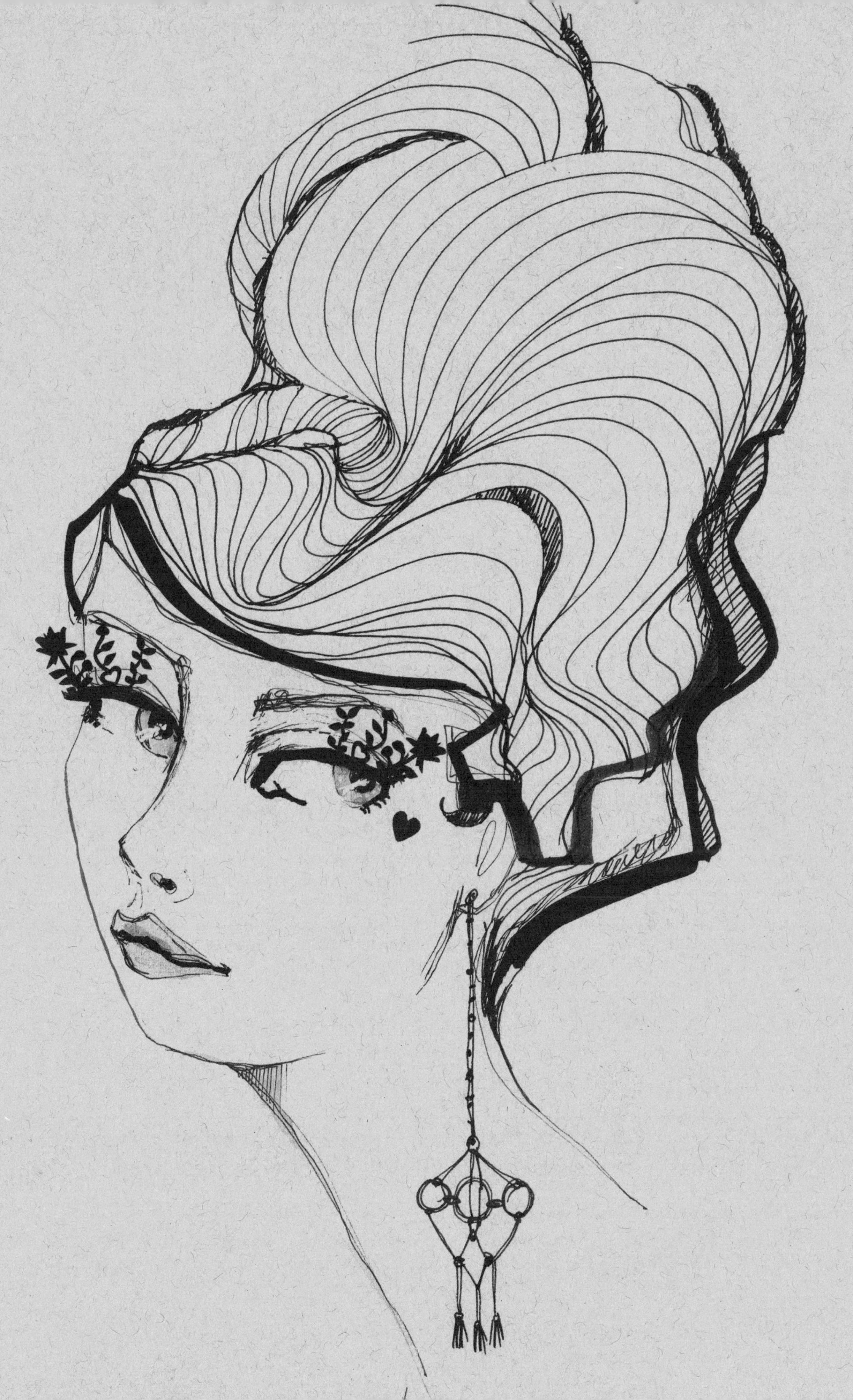

we are

spinning

LIKE

mad

confetti

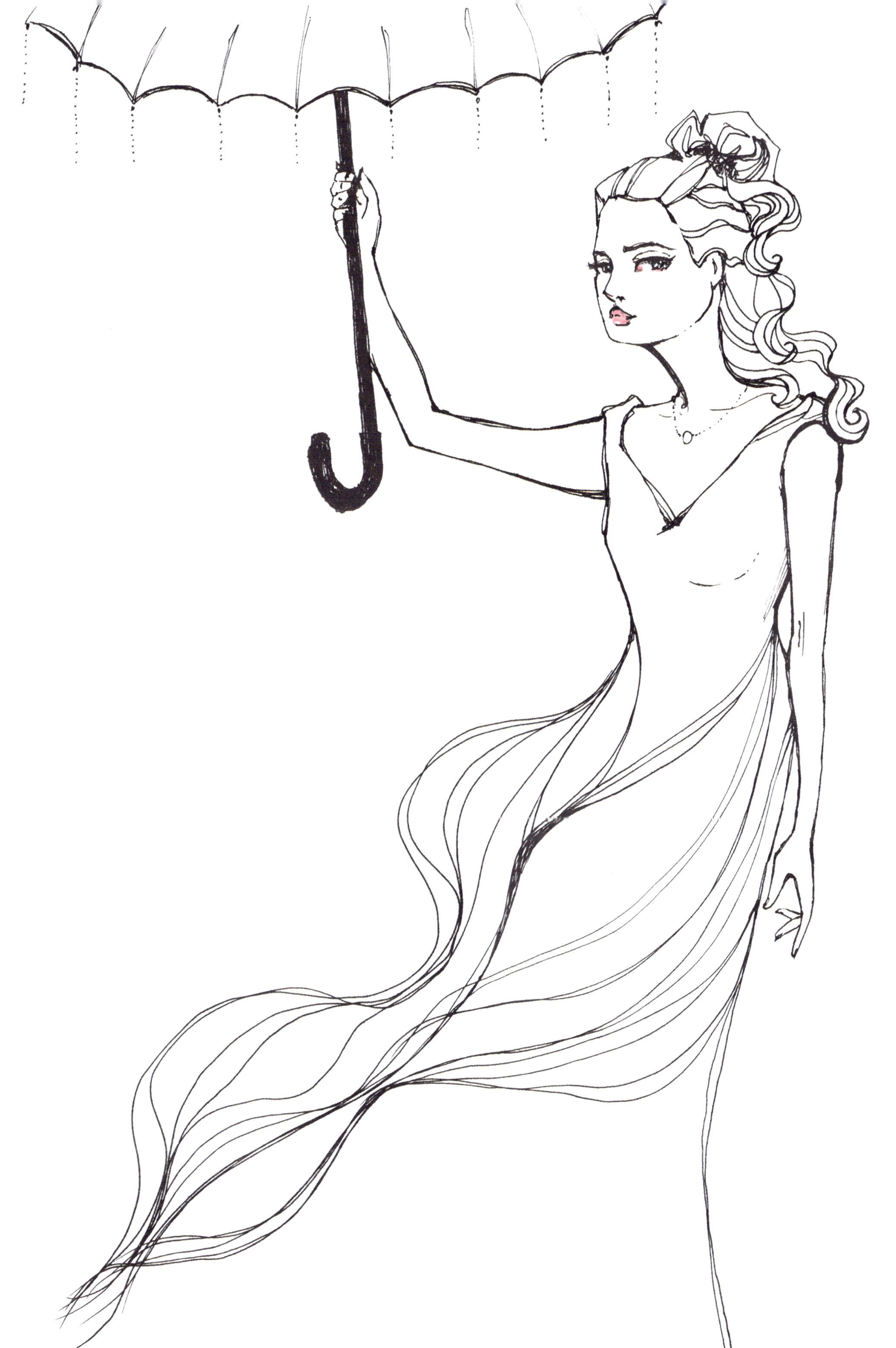

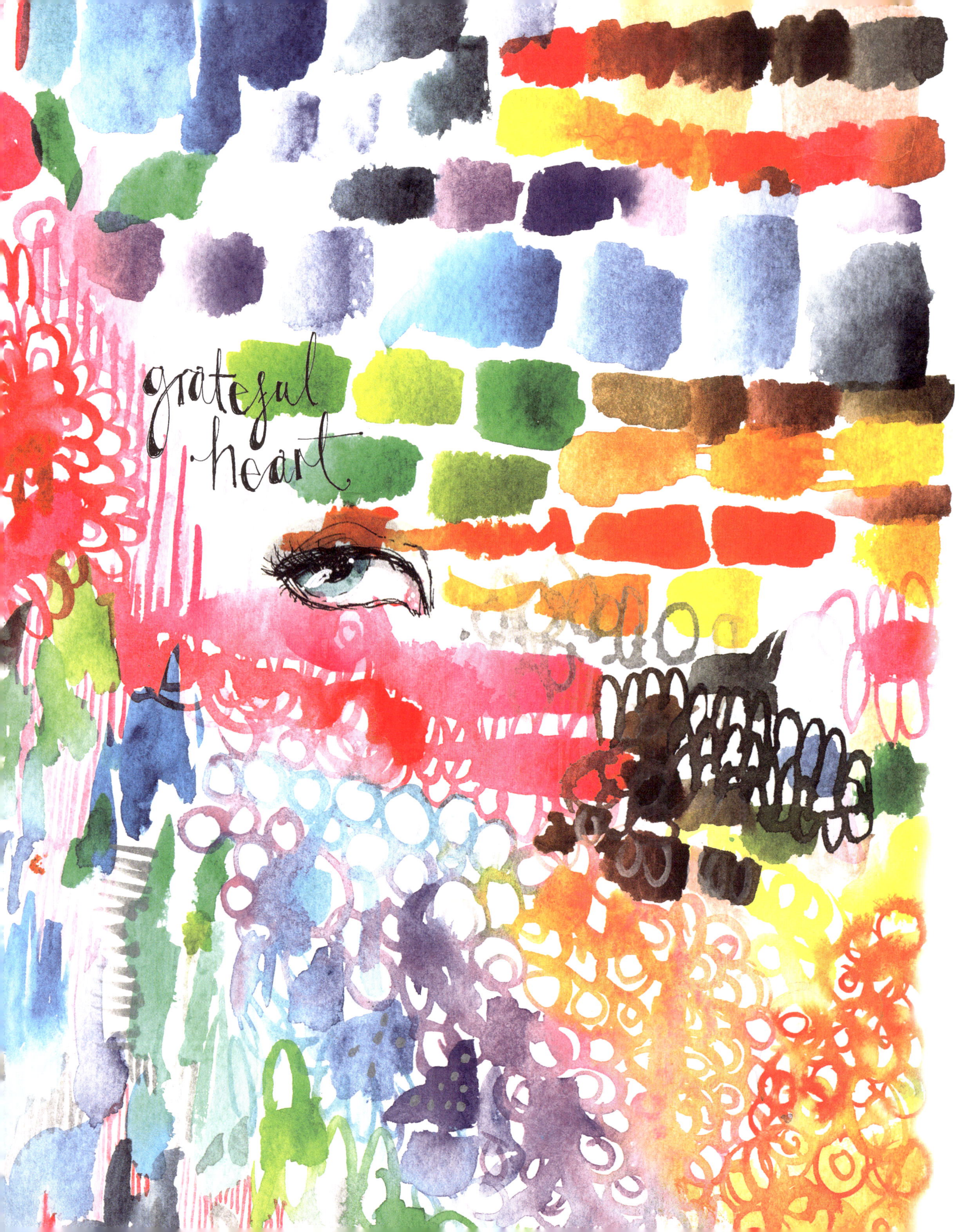

grateful heart

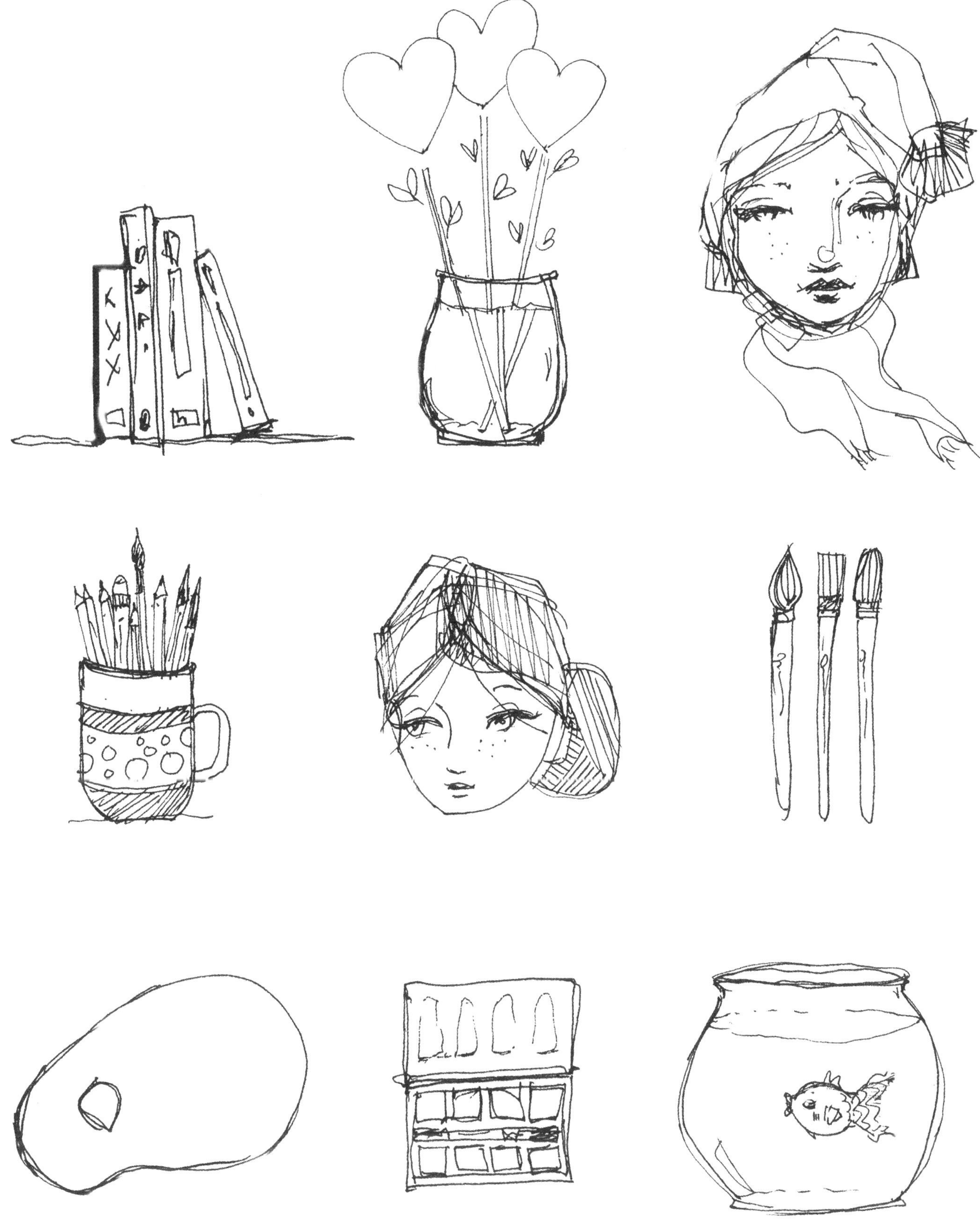

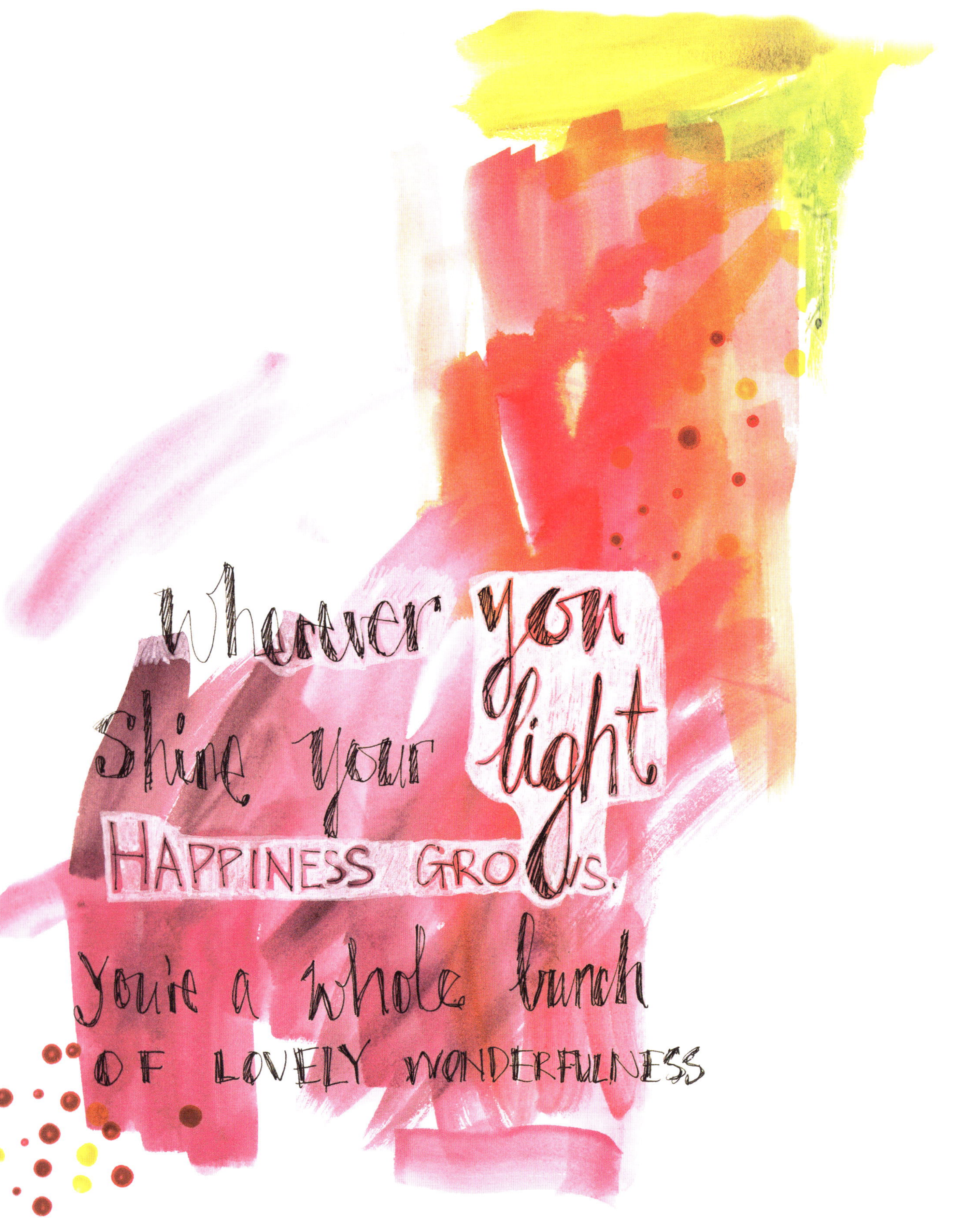

Wherever you shine your light
HAPPINESS GROWS.
You're a whole bunch
OF LOVELY WONDERFULNESS

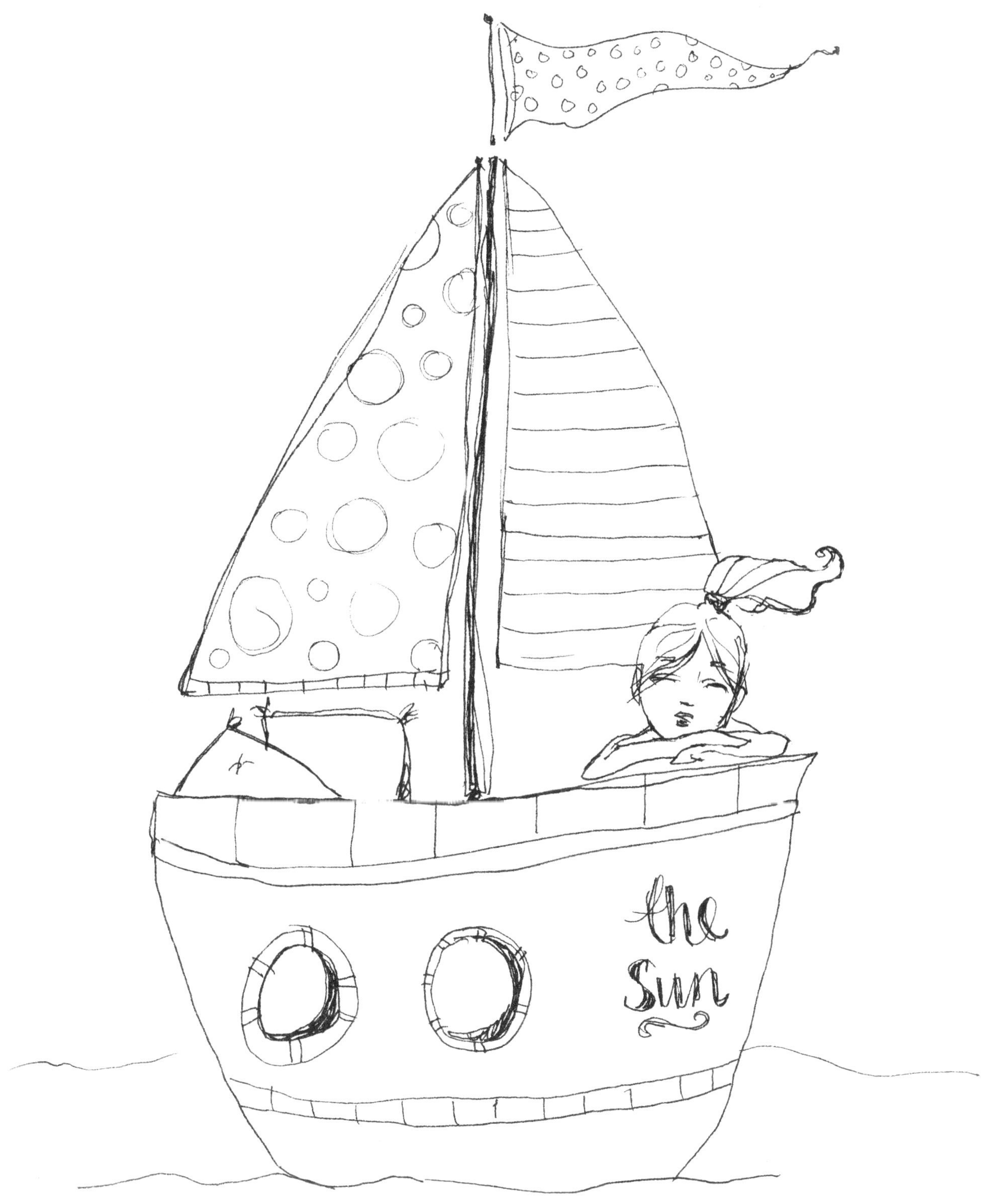
the
Sun

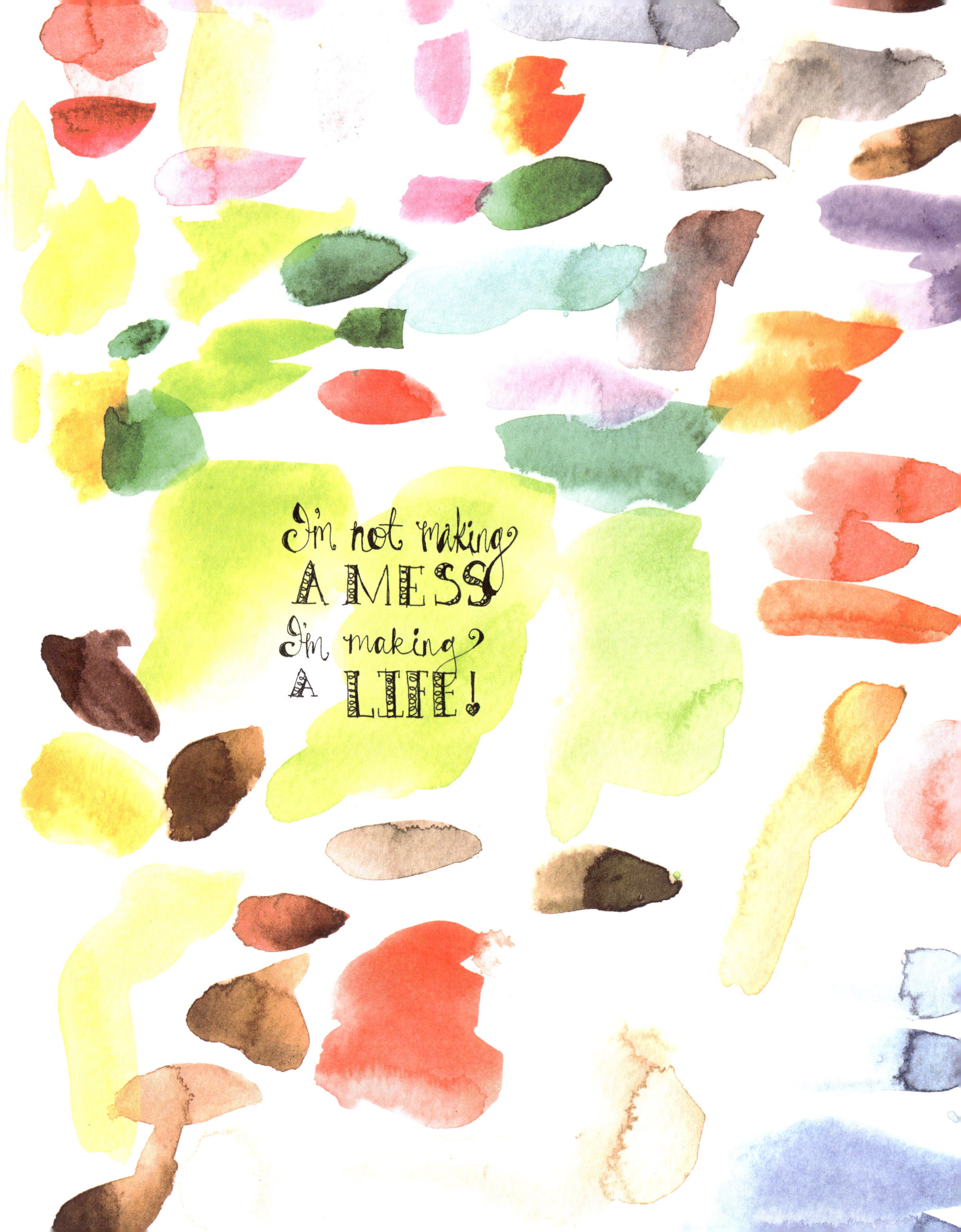

I'm not making
A MESS
I'm making
A LIFE!

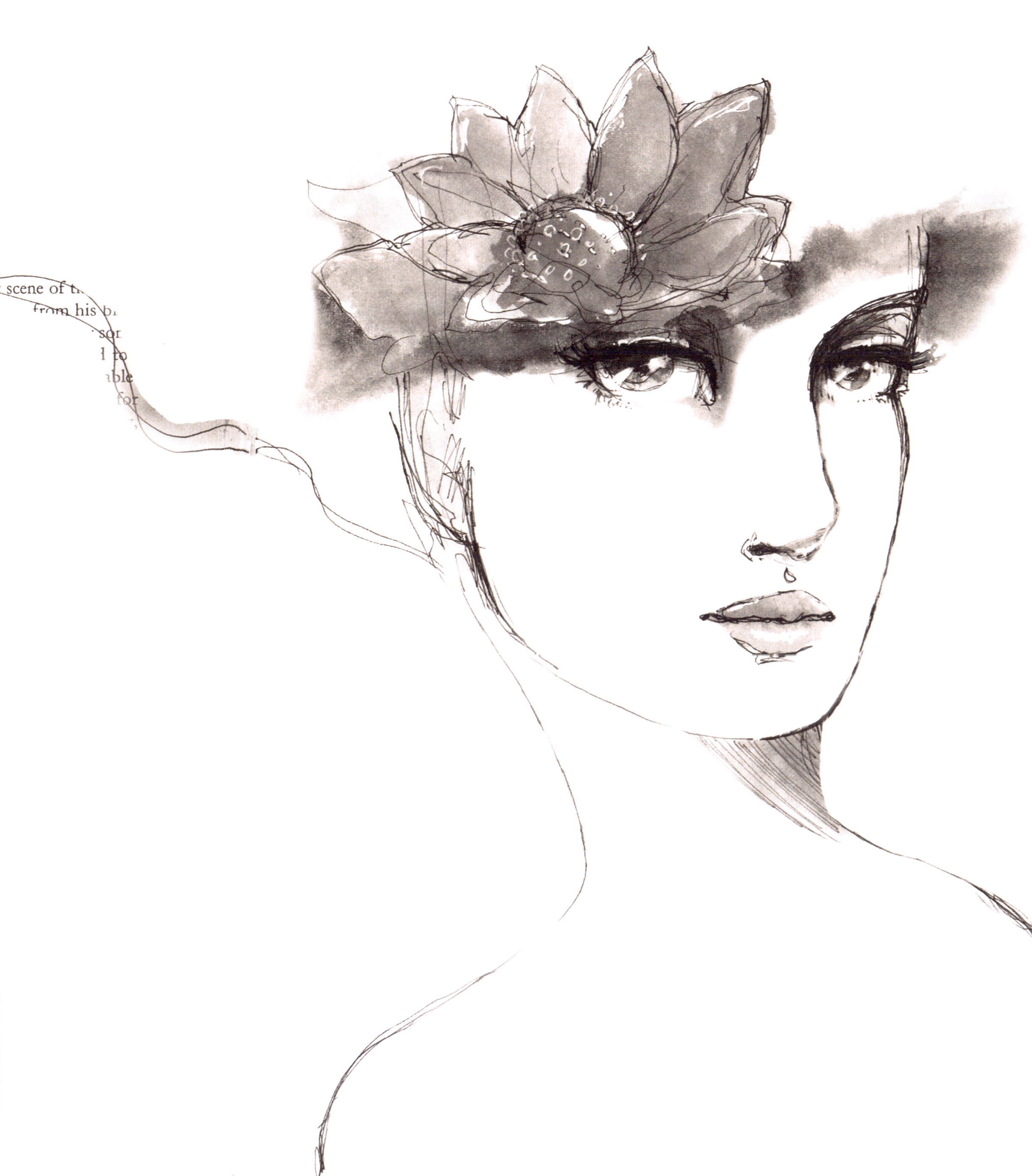

scene of t
from his b
sor
l to
ble
for

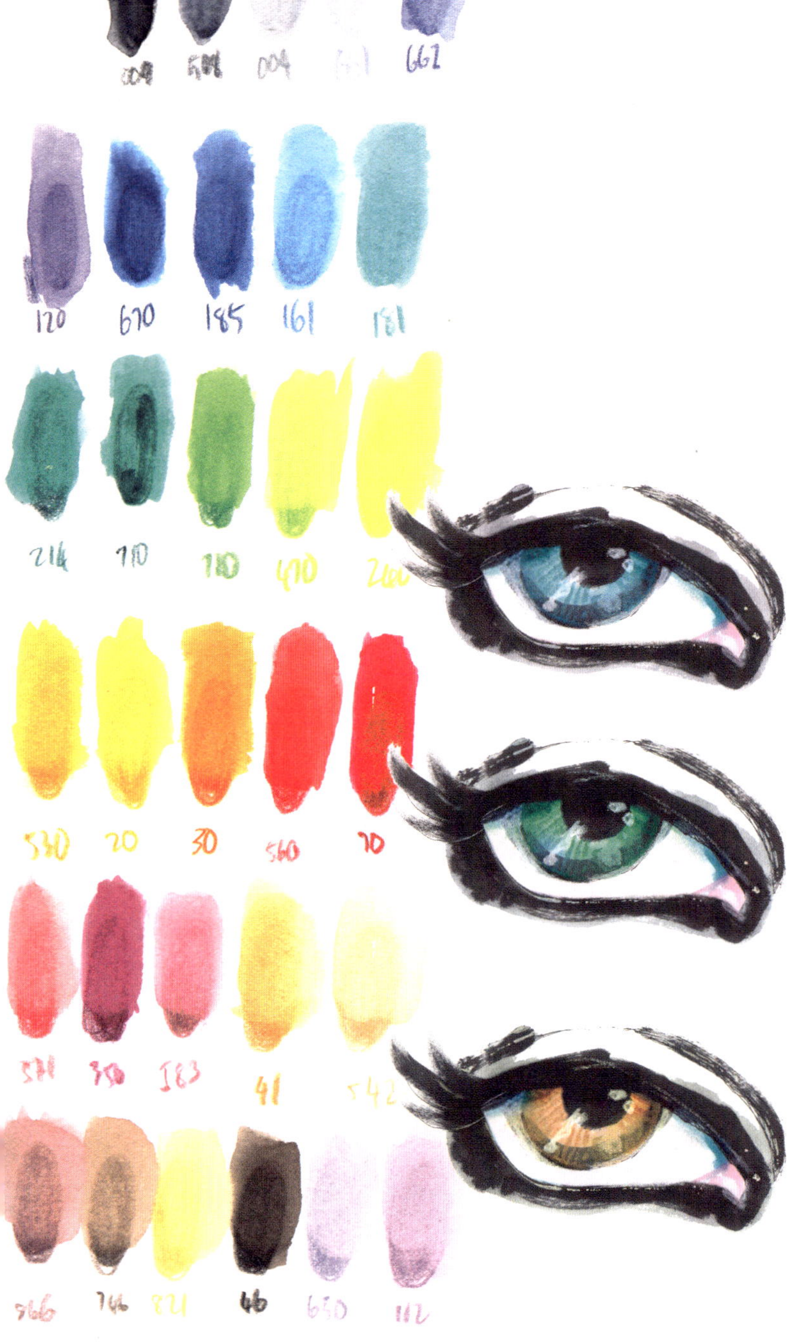

when they told me "NO"
I thought "for you maybe,
but not for me."

CYNDI LAUPER

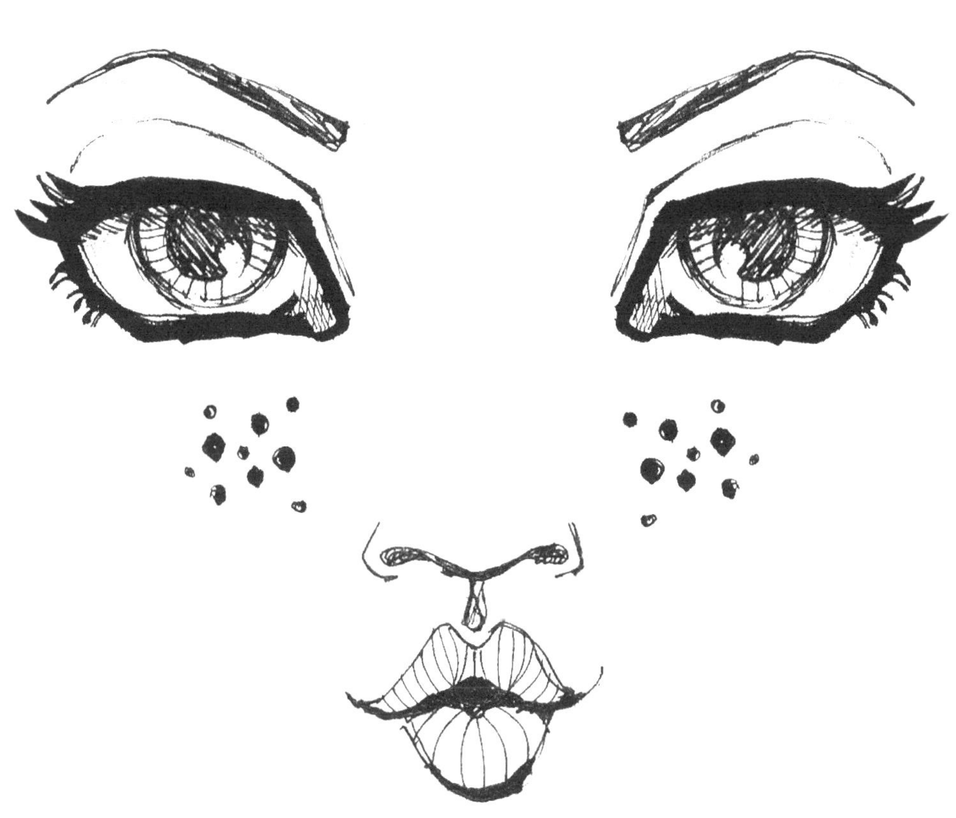

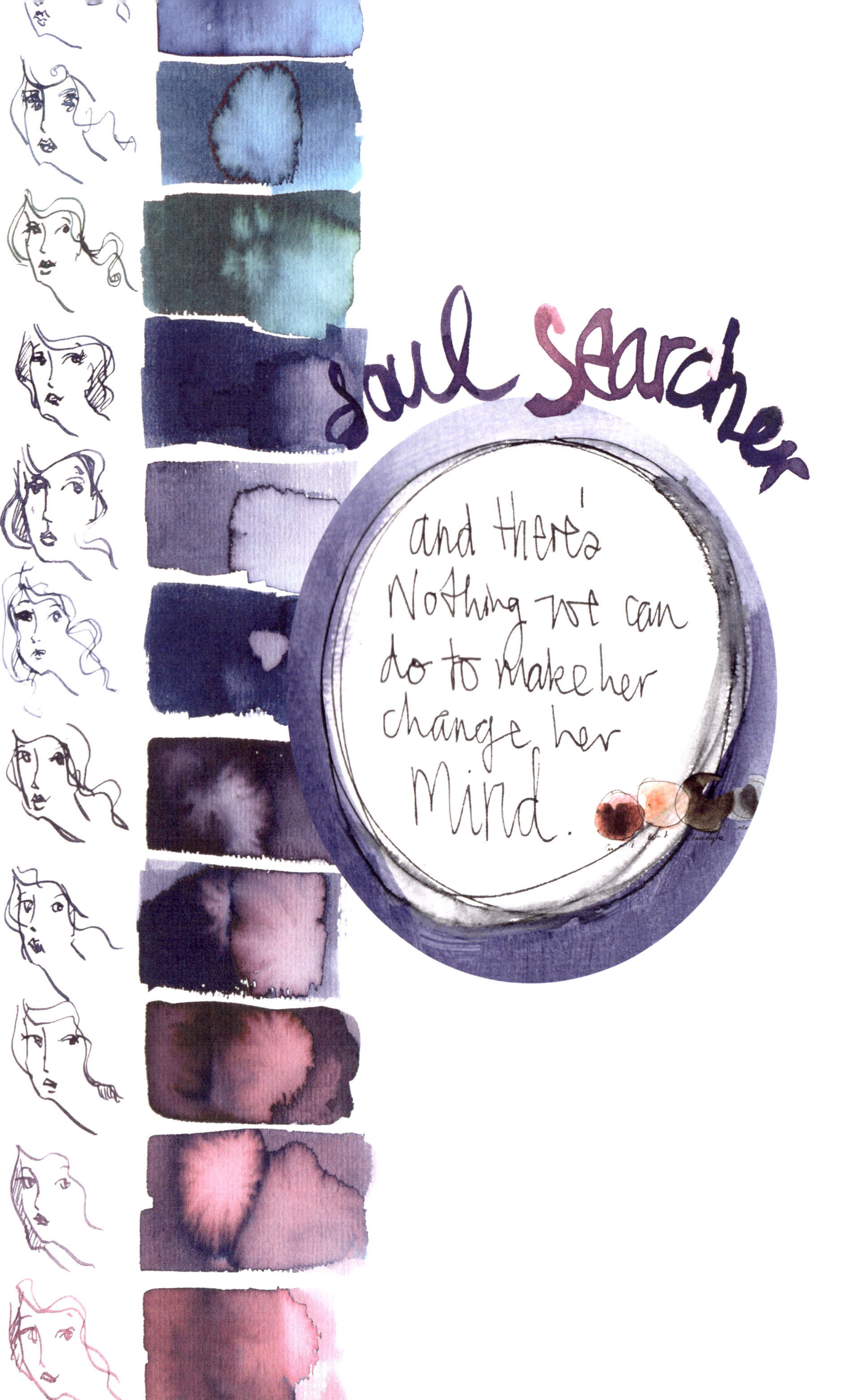
Soul Searcher
and there's
Nothing you can
do to make her
change her
Mind.

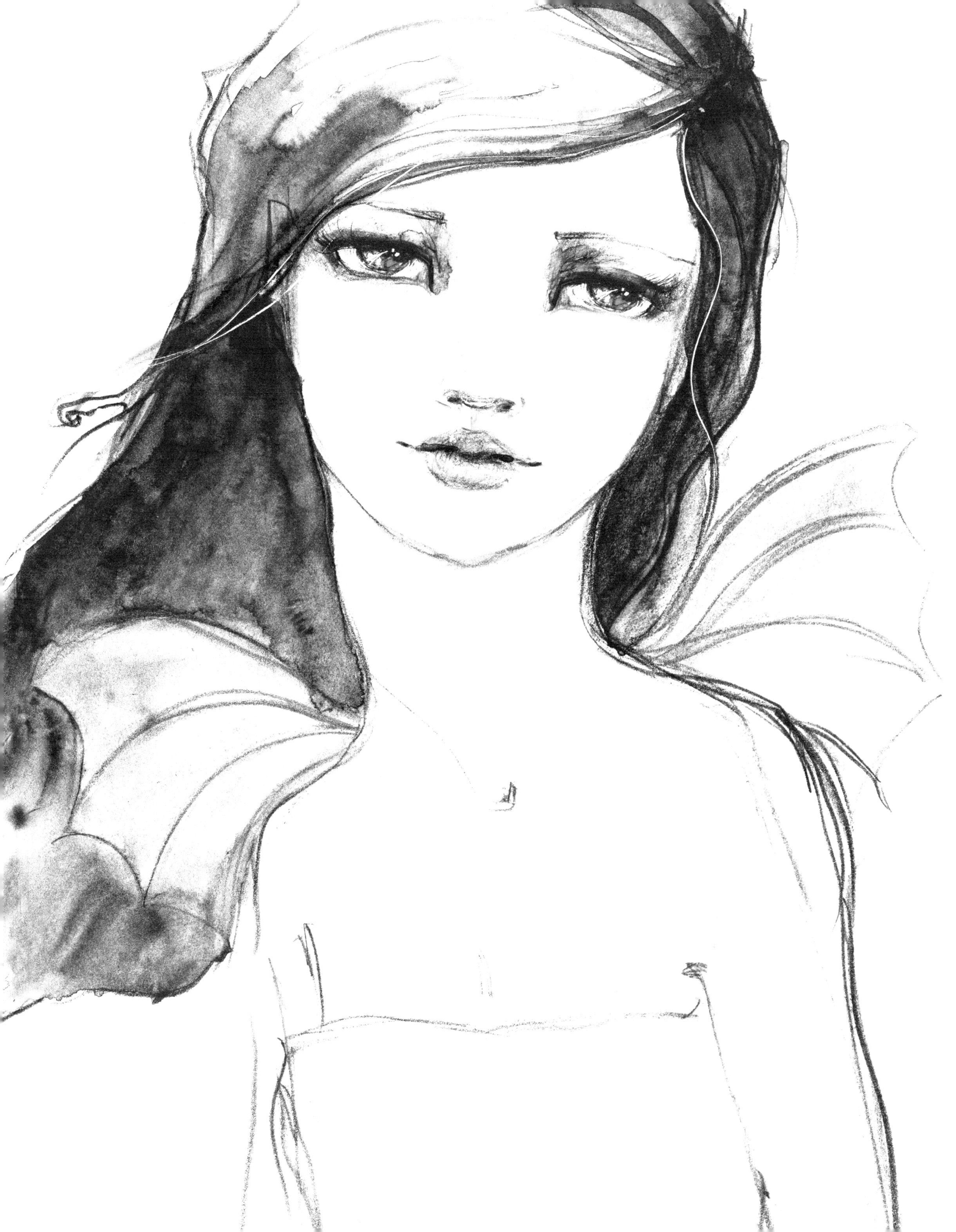

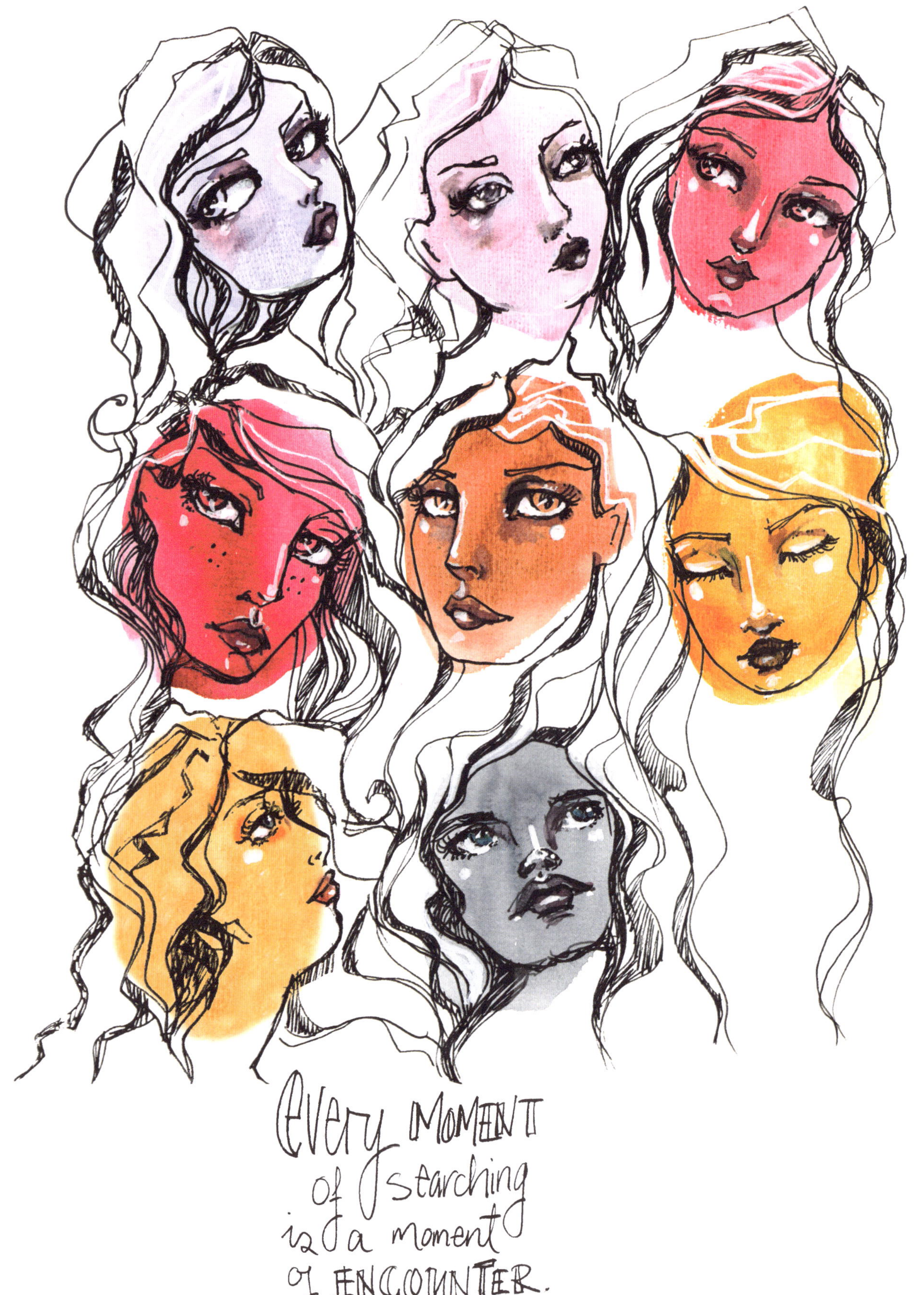

every MOMENT
of searching
is a moment
of ENCOUNTER.
PAUL COELHO

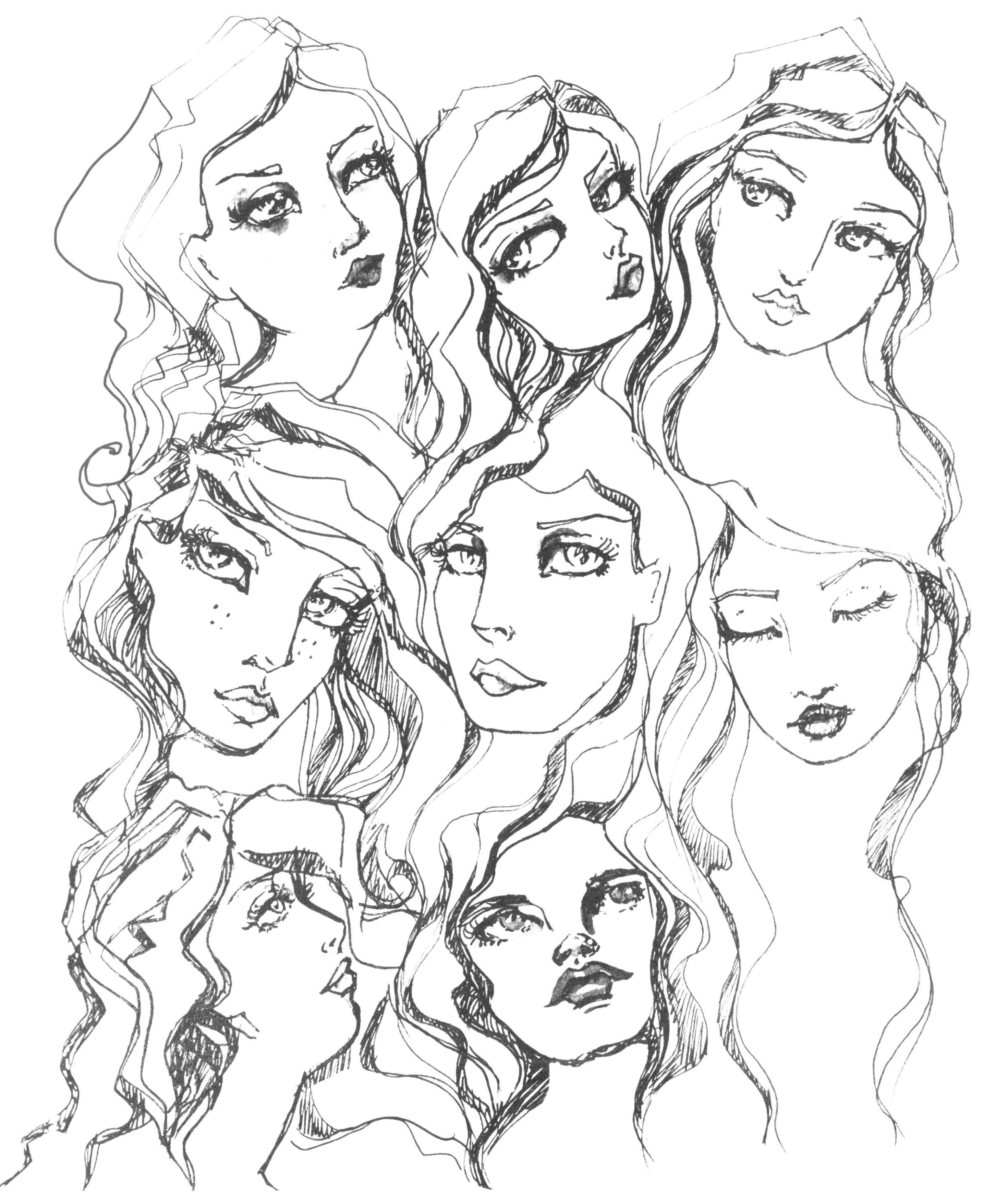

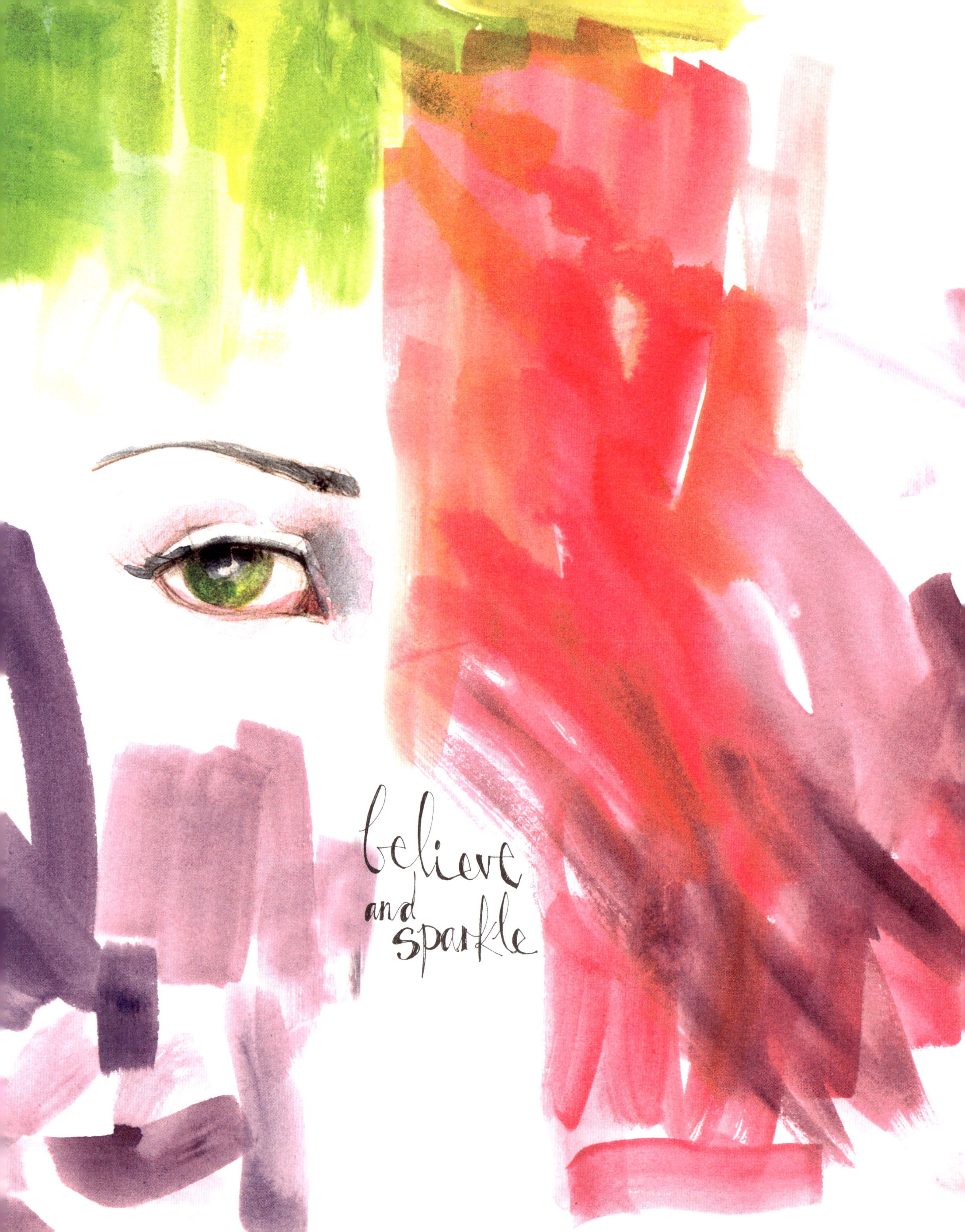
believe
and
sparkle

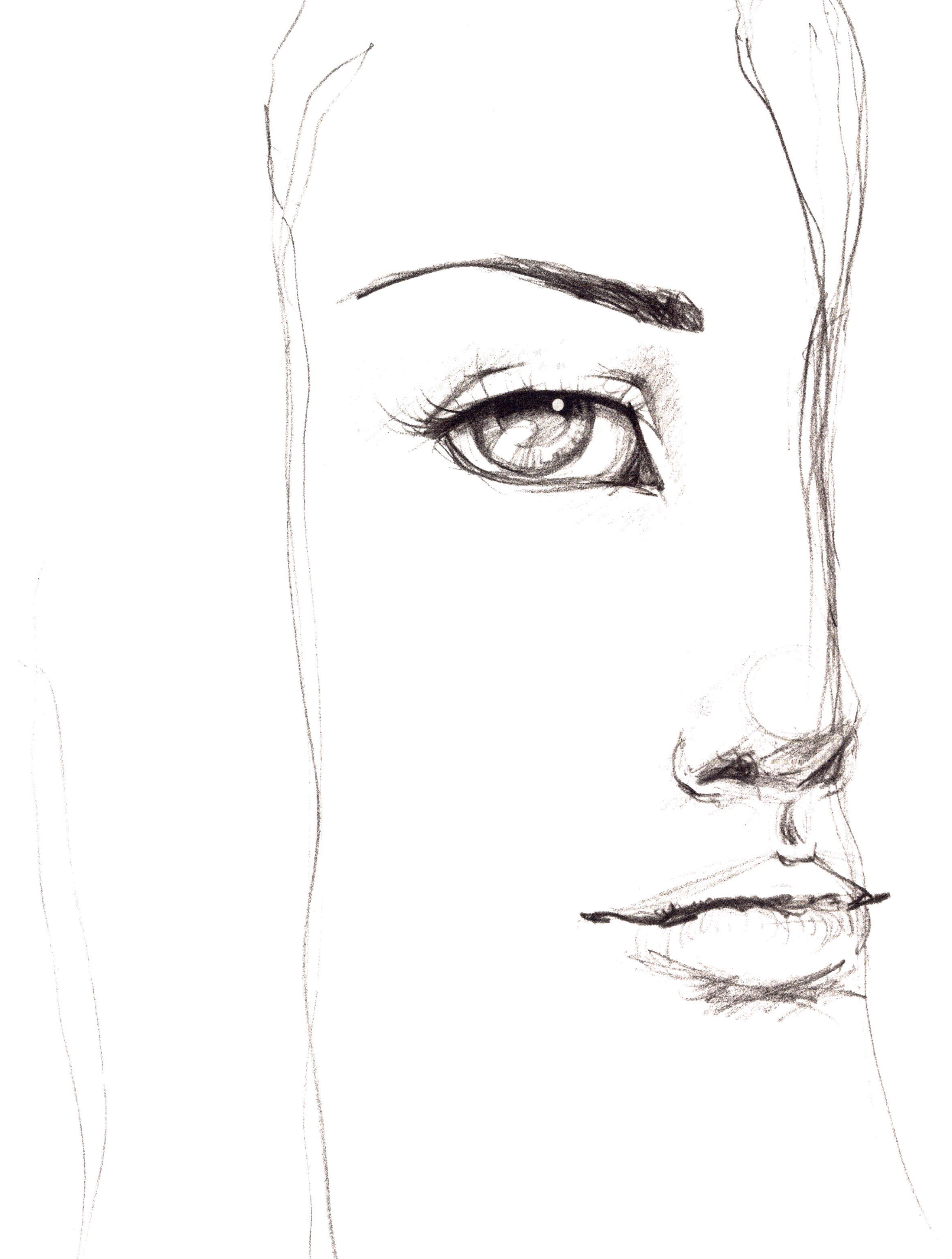

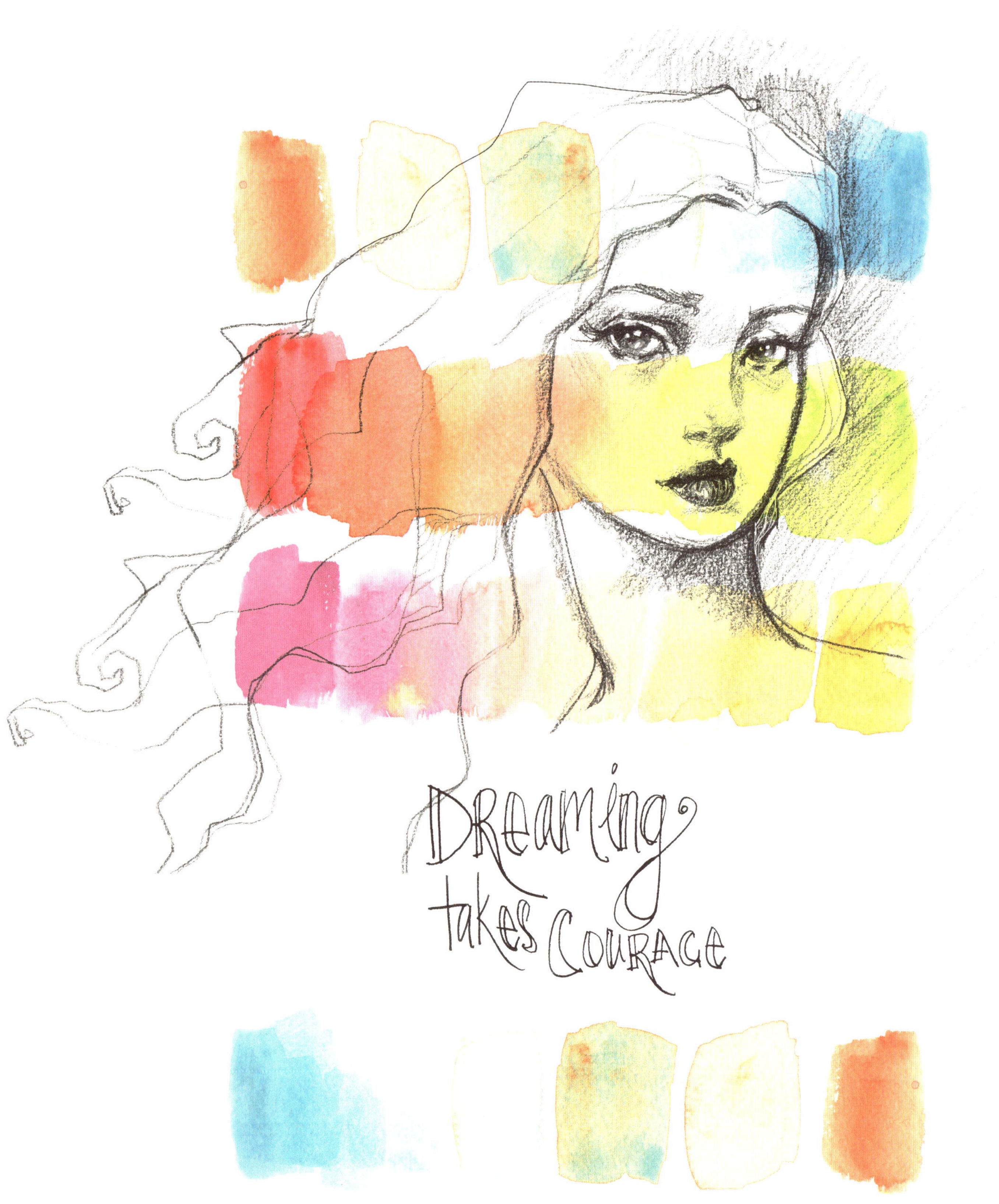

Dreaming
takes Courage

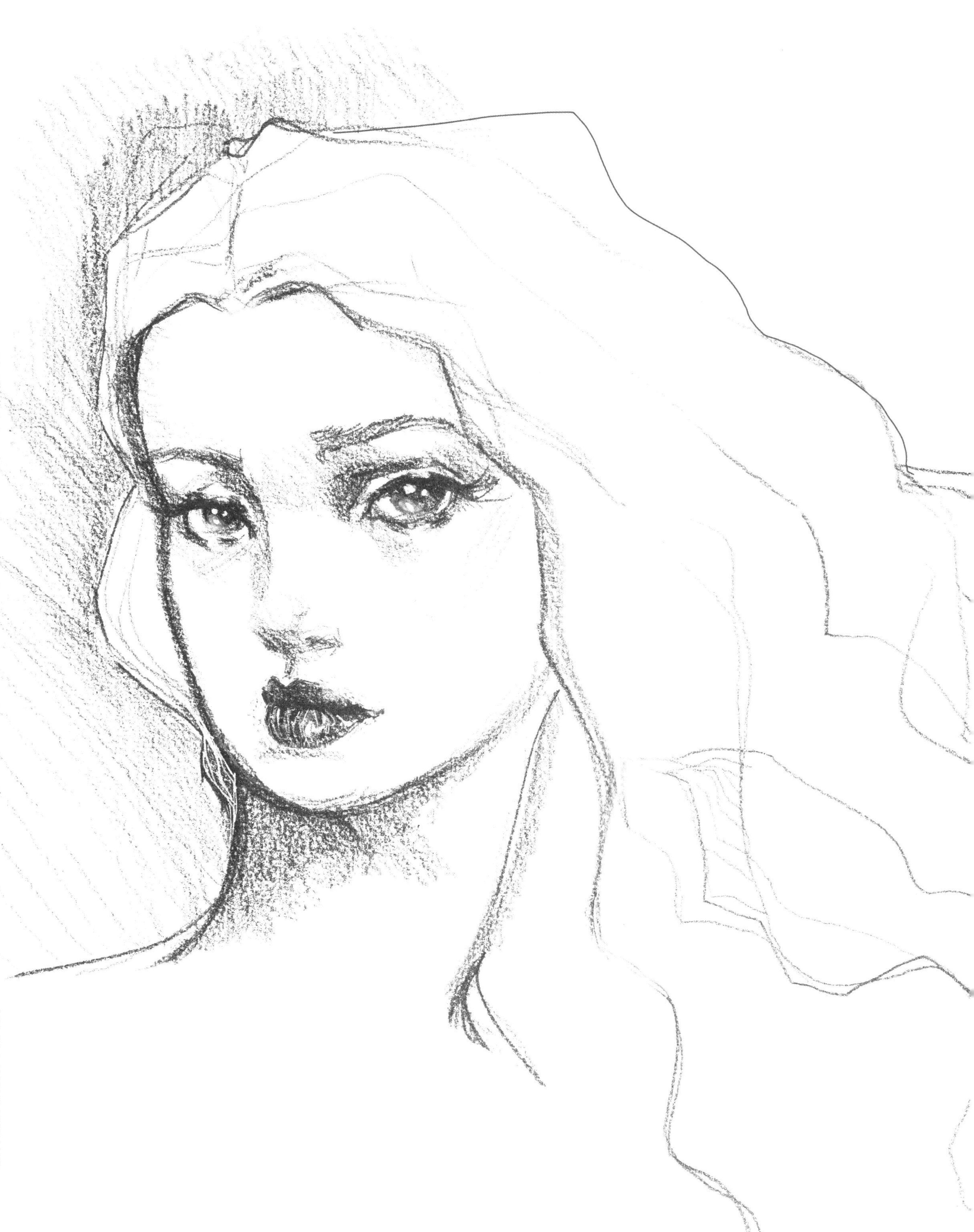

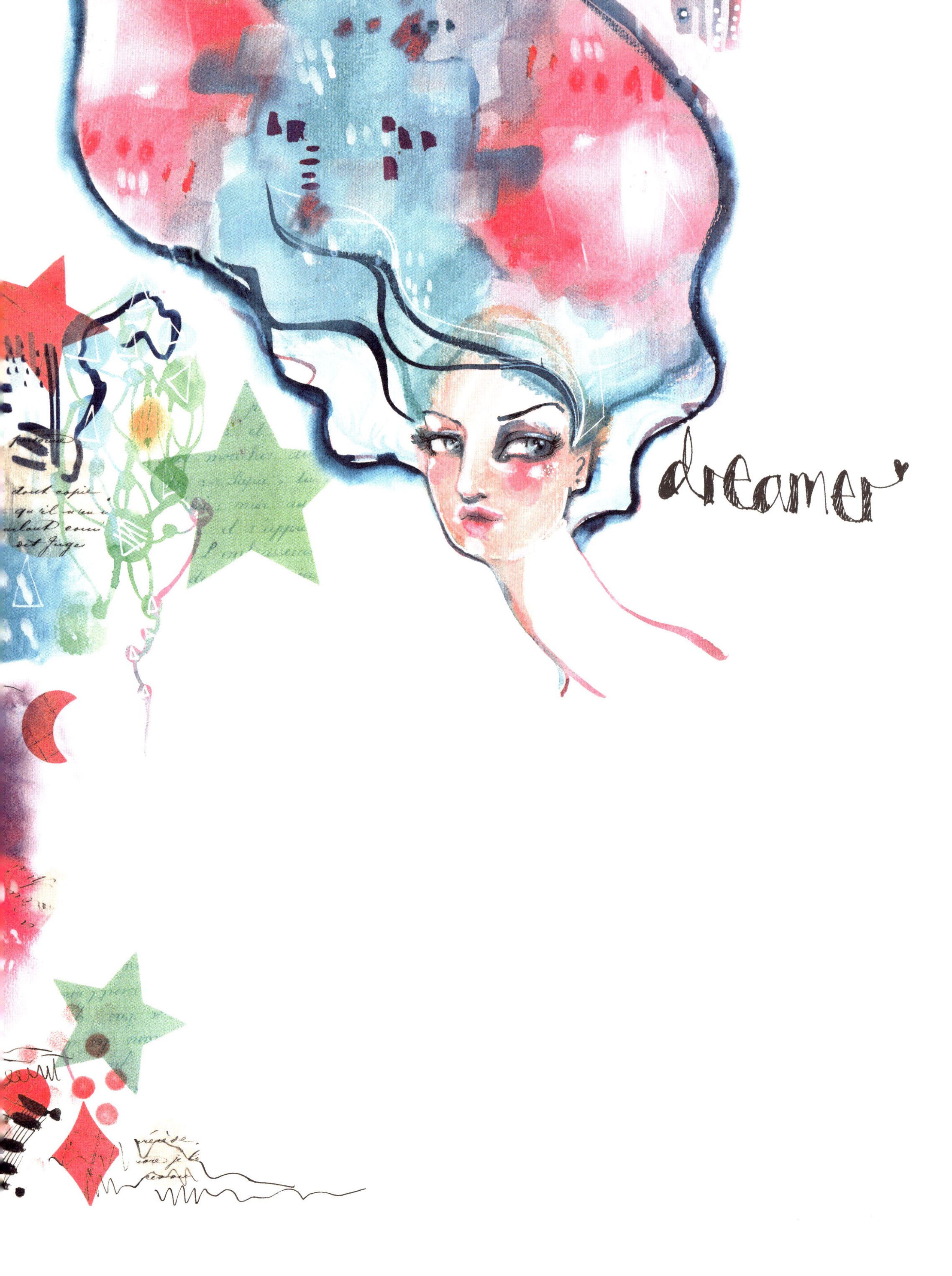

dreamer

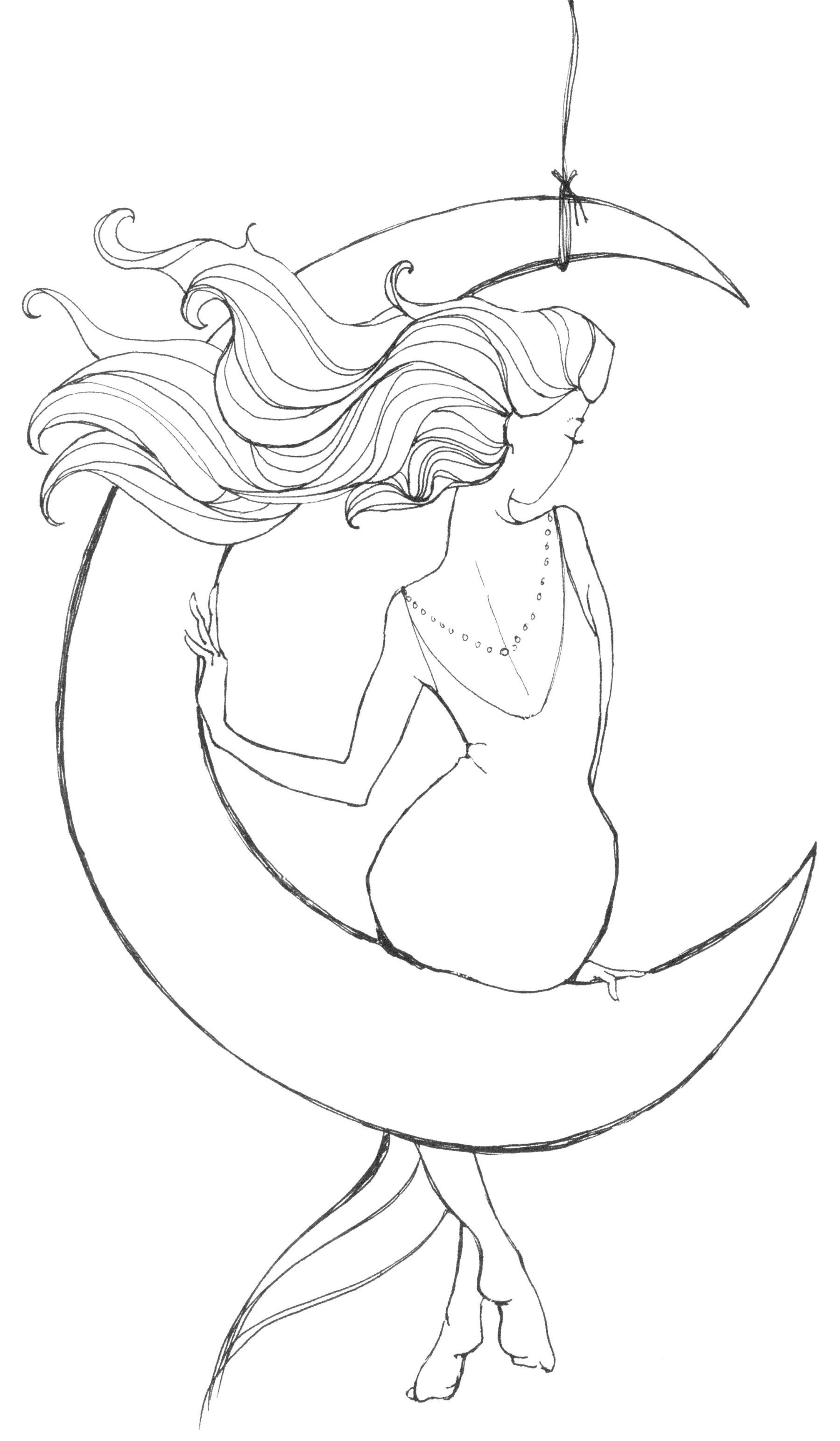

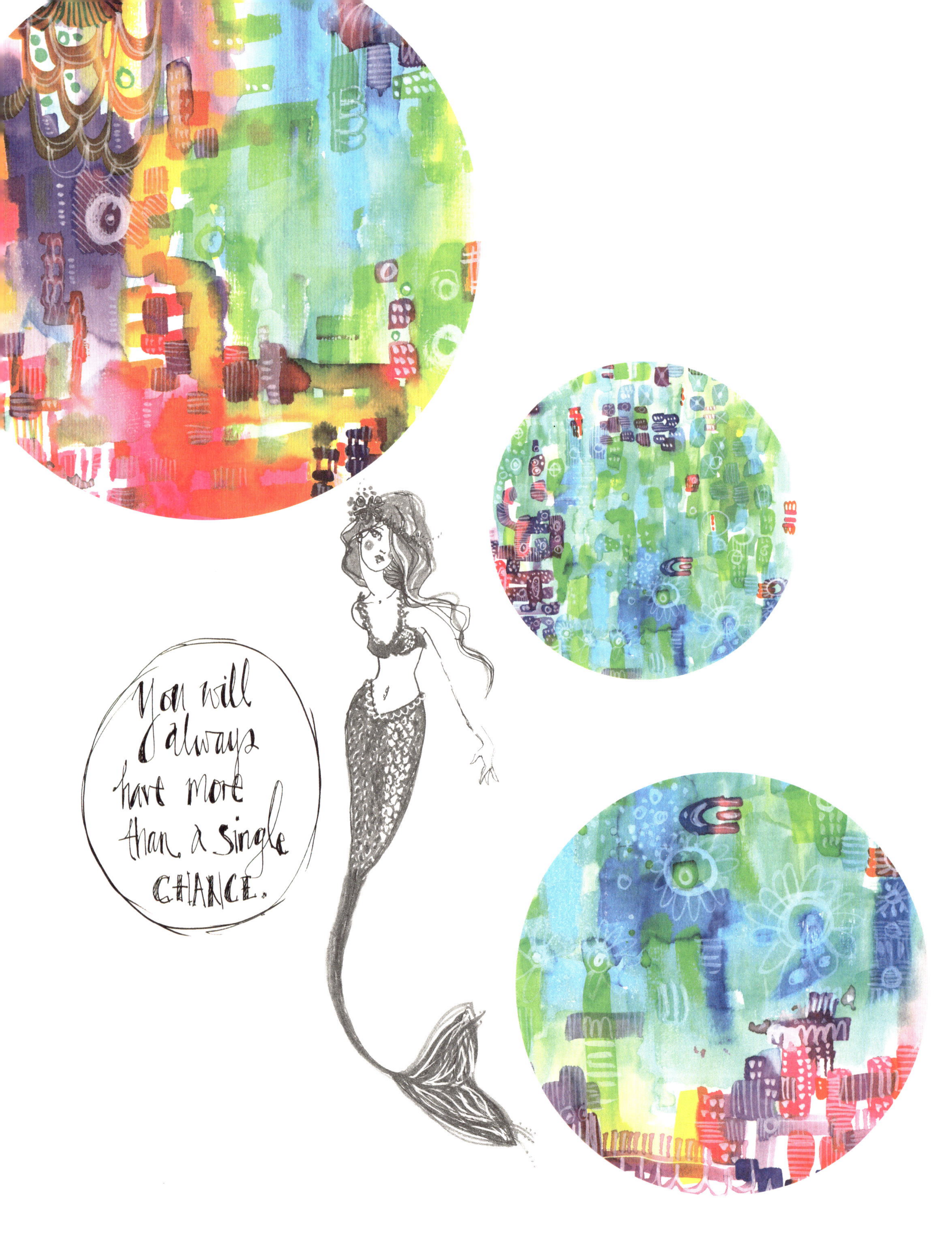
You will always have more than a single CHANCE.

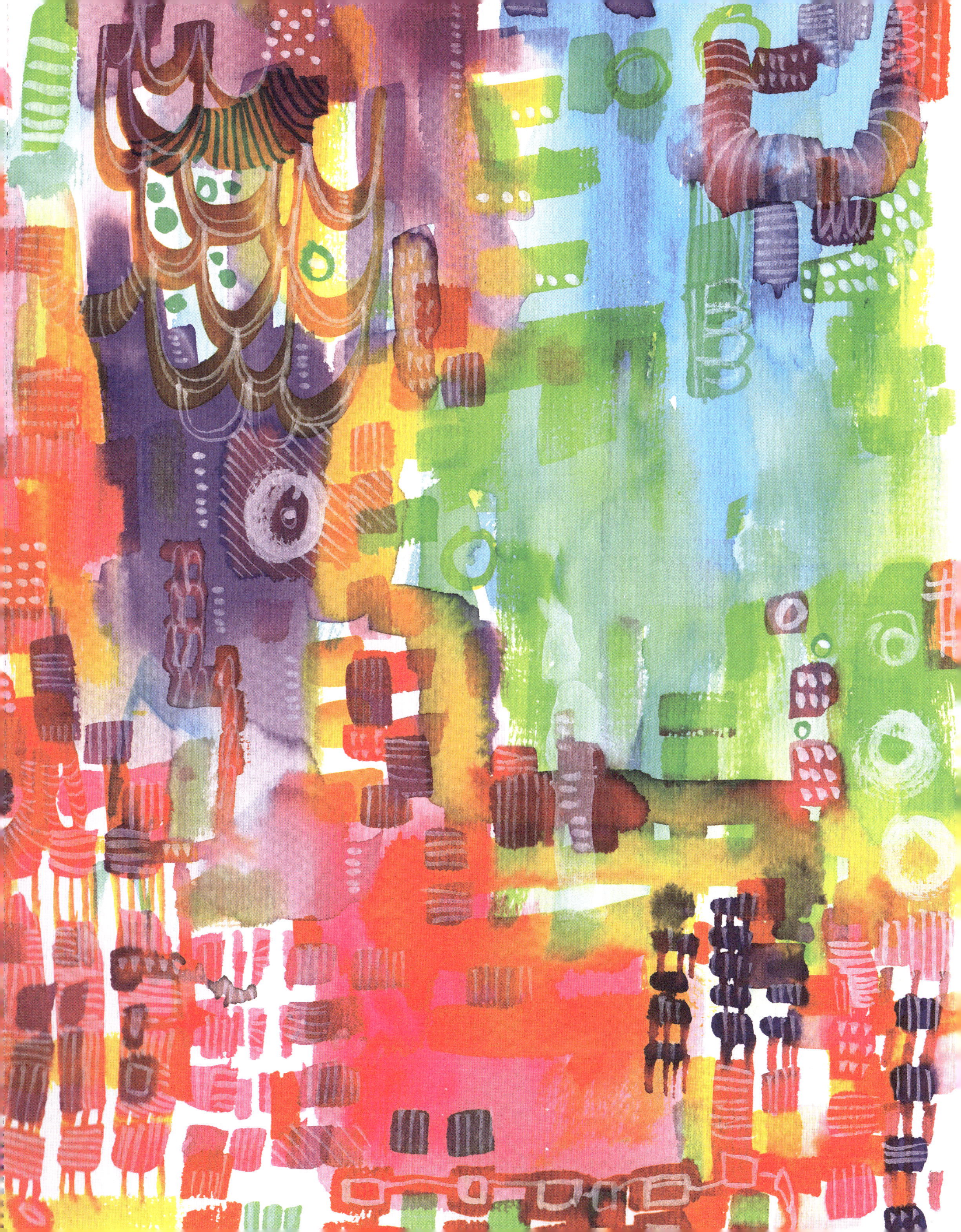

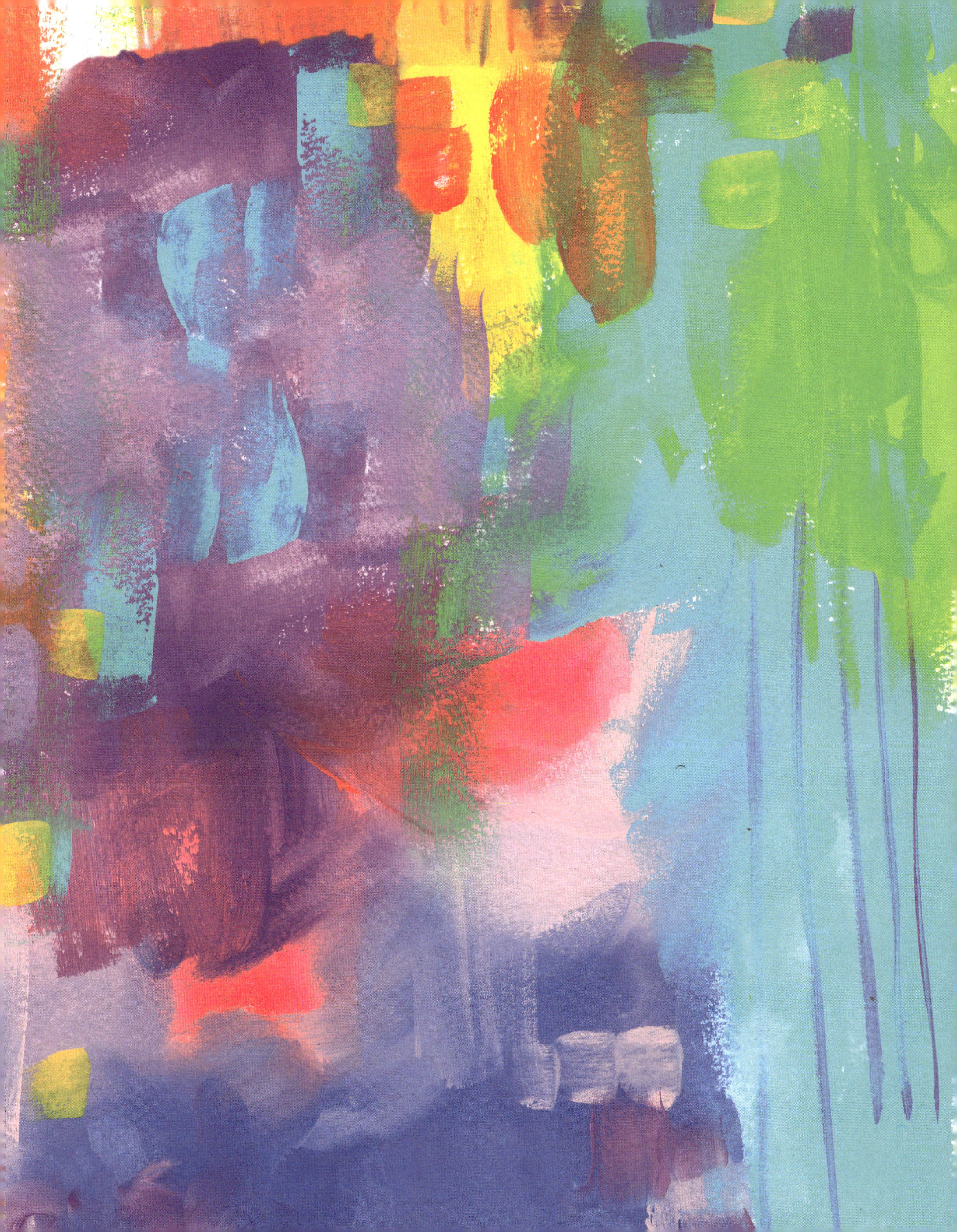